Kids Taking Action

Community Service Learning Projects, K–8

Pamela Roberts

with contributions from Alice Yang

ISBN 1-892989-07-7

Library of Congress catalog card number 2002101349

Photo on page 38 courtesy of *Daily Hampshire Gazette.*

Photo on page 102 by Steve Simonsen.

Other photos courtesy of Pamela Roberts, Karen Lefave, Marika Roth, Kathy Struck, Kate Foley, Mike Feldstein, Joan Godsey, Monita Leavitt, Michele Hebert, Bill Limero, Chris Wings, and Victoria Roberts-Wierzbowski.

Northeast Foundation for Children
39 Montague City Road
Greenfield, MA 01301
(800) 360-6332
www.responsiveclassroom.org

Printed in Canada

Acknowledgments

I would like to thank the following people for their help with this book:

Alice Yang, writer/editor at Northeast Foundation for Children (NEFC), who shepherded this book from the earliest research through to final manuscript. Her thoughtful and careful editing helped give the book breadth and shape. In addition, she researched and wrote the thirteen projects-at-a-glance.

Lynn Bechtel, writer/editor at NEFC, who copyedited the manuscript and coordinated production of the book.

Roxann Kriete, executive director of NEFC, whose vision and encouragement got the project off the ground. Her view of the larger purpose and her guidance along the way helped make this project a success.

Jay Lord, co-founder of NEFC, who urged me to submit a book proposal on community service learning.

Mary Beth Forton, editorial director at NEFC, who reviewed the manuscript in its various stages and offered valuable feedback.

Michael Fleck, whose careful proofreading gave the manuscript its final polish.

All the teachers, educators, and students who so graciously took the time to share their experiences and thoughts about community service learning. They are the heart of this book.

This book is dedicated to my two children,
Thomas and Victoria Roberts-Wierzbowski.

Contents

What Is Community Service Learning?

My introduction to community service learning (CSL) came in the fall of 1999. I was a parent helping with a community service project at Greenfield Center School, the independent K–8 school established by Northeast Foundation for Children in Greenfield, Massachusetts.

That fall, students in two combined fifth-sixth grade classes made fleece hats and gave them to local children in need of warm clothing. It was a very successful community service project. The students learned a skill, how to use a sewing machine, and more importantly, they contributed something tangible and useful to others. They even received recognition from the press for their efforts.

However, when one of the teachers and I discussed the project afterwards, we agreed that something was missing. Some of the students just didn't "get" it. They were making the hats because the teacher told them to, not because they saw a need to help. They hadn't fully understood the rationale behind the project, which was that some families can't afford the warm clothing needed for New England winters. And, the project had been separate from their "real" work, their curriculum.

That was when I discovered how community service differs from community service learning, which combines students' service to the community with academic learning. CSL teaches civic responsibility while involving students in active learning. For a project to be truly service learning, there needs to be both a community service goal and a learning goal, with time for students to reflect upon both aspects.

"[CSL is] different from community service, which is doing something for others, because of the primary curricular piece," said Laura Baker, principal of Greenfield Center School. Whereas a community service project might replace an academic segment of the day, a community service learning project is part of it. "CSL is one element of the curriculum instead of separate from it," says Baker.

A small addition to more conventional activities

Sometimes a small change is all that's needed to turn service into service learning. With the fleece hat project, for example, Baker suggested tying in a study of weather and its effects on people. Depending on the class's curriculum, this weather study might help students meet goals in science and social studies. For example, students could learn, among other things, that extreme heat and extreme cold can be especially dangerous for two populations—the elderly and children.

Similarly, traditional classroom learning can often be turned into a service learning project with a modest addition. Baker described a monarch butterfly study that was part of the combined third-fourth grade curriculum at Shutesbury Elementary School in Shutesbury, Massachusetts, where she was formerly principal. While doing their research, the students found an organization that tracks monarch butterflies. The students began to tag the butterflies and list the butterfly numbers on the Internet. Suddenly, they were making a real contribution to the scientific community. The addition of this one piece—tagging the butterflies—turned the academic project into a service learning project. "It was so exciting," Baker said, "because it made the learning real."

From isolated efforts to an organized movement

The idea behind CSL is not new. For years, many teachers and schools across the country have been engaging students in projects that benefit the community while enhancing students' academic skills. They may not have called their work "community service learning." Nonetheless, their good work has improved communities and changed lives.

In recent years CSL has grown from isolated efforts by individual teachers into a movement embraced by much of the educational and political establishment. In 1990, the federal government formed a commission that provides grants and other assistance to service programs, including school-based ones. In 1993, the federal role was expanded with the creation of the Corporation for National Service, which provides funds for every state to bring service learning into K–12 education.

Efforts at the state level have also mushroomed. Nearly all states, with support from the Corporation for National Service, are administering service learning programs through their state education agencies, and many states are supplementing federal money with funds of their own. As of 2001, six states (Idaho, Michigan, Minnesota, New Jersey, New Mexico, and Vermont) included service learning in the state's education standards. Seven states allowed participation in service learning to be applied toward graduation requirements, and one (Maryland) required service learning for graduation. (Compact for Learning and Citizenship 2001, 2) In addition, numerous school districts have been working to institutionalize CSL so that it becomes an integral and consistent part of school.

Meanwhile, the private sector has joined in, with one of the more notable efforts being the W. K. Kellogg Foundation's Learning In Deed initiative. Begun in 1998, the four-year, $13 million effort aims to work with teachers, administrators, community members, parents, students, policy makers, and national leaders to develop sound CSL policies, practices, research, and leadership.

With such a concerted push, the number of students involved in CSL has grown. According to a U. S. Department of Education survey, thirty-two percent of all public schools in the nation had students participating in service learning in 1999, including twenty-five percent of elementary schools and thirty-eight percent of middle schools. (National Center for Education Statistics 1999, 5) The same survey found that more than eight out of ten schools with service learning programs offer some kind of support to teachers interested in doing CSL projects. The types of support include sending teachers to training outside of the school, providing grants to cover the costs of service learning projects, offering extra planning time for service-learning activities, and having a full-time service learning coordinator on staff. (National Center for Education Statistics 1999, 9)

For teachers, all this is welcome news. The increased financial and practical support aside, these recent developments represent a renewed appreciation and honoring of teachers' efforts to help children be good students, good citizens, and good human beings.

I hope this book will help you. The strategies it presents, the profiles of actual CSL projects, and the voices of the teachers and students involved are meant to offer ideas that you can adapt to best meet your purposes. As you'll see in the pages that follow, CSL can work—for you, your students, and your community.

References:

Compact for Learning and Citizenship, Education Commission of the States. 2001. "Institutionalized Service-Learning in the 50 States." *ECS State Notes, Service-Learning Policy Scan* (March).

National Center for Education Statistics. 1999. "Service-Learning and Community Service in K–12 Public Schools." *Statistics in Brief.* (September) Publication number NCES 1999-043.

Benefits of Community Service Learning

Community service learning provides an authentic way to teach and learn, making it very appealing to many teachers. Although CSL often involves more initial work than traditional classroom lessons, educators report that the investment of time is worthwhile because the payoffs are so rich for everyone—teachers, students, schools, and communities. Here are some of the most important benefits of CSL:

CSL engages children in active learning.

Community service learning requires students to take action, whether they're writing letters in support of a cause, cleaning up a playground, or conducting a voter registration drive. It also requires a high level of personal engagement: instead of being passive recipients of education, students learn from the experience of trying to solve real-world problems. As fifth grade teacher Joan Godsey said about her class's project of raising salmon for release into the Connecticut River, "To me, CSL is the best kind of learning. You study and understand a concept, then you do it hands-on." When learning comes alive like this, students feel more interested and invested in school.

A variety of academic subjects can be plugged into a single community service learning project. In general, the more integrated into the curriculum a project is, the deeper the learning and understanding become. In an annual quilt project in Massachusetts, kindergartners make quilts for babies who are in a homeless shelter. In the process, the students arrange quilt squares, examine fabric, read books about quilt-making, learn about the family and historical themes that frequently appear on quilts, and write their hopes for the babies. Through these activities, the students learn and practice skills in math, language arts, social studies, and science.

CSL helps children understand what it means to be part of a community.

Students examine concepts of community through two levels of involvement. There is the community within which students work and learn, usually the classroom, as they undertake a CSL project. Interacting with each other and their teacher as they work on the project, students build relationships, become a more cohesive unit, and gain a sense of group identity.

There is also the community that the students serve. As children work to help their school, neighborhood, town, a more distant place, or the natural world, they develop a relationship with that community and a feeling of membership in it. Children also begin to understand that they are part of many different communities.

CSL teaches children how to be good citizens in a democracy.

Democracy is based on the notion that people have a say in their lives and that they help each other. As Larry Dieringer, executive director of Educators for Social Responsibility, puts it, "Democracy is something we need to do, not something we have." CSL gives students the skills they need to do democracy, to be active citizens.

Through their participation in CSL projects, children see that they can make a difference. James C. Kielsmeier, founder and president of the National Youth Leadership Council, writes, "As students enter classrooms to teach other students, as they research their past and make contributions to history, as they bring visibility and change to an environmental issue, they are citizens today—not just the promise of tomorrow." (Kielsmeier 2000, 657) Even the youngest of children can be "citizens today." After completing a project with her class to make their school playground safe from dog droppings, one first grader said, "It made me feel if you have a good fight and you work hard, you can do something important, even if you're small." (Ratner 1997)

CSL instills an ethic of service.

Most educators agree that children want to do good and will act on that desire if given the chance. CSL gives children this chance. "Community service learning promotes the development of a social conscience in young people," says Sheldon Berman, superintendent of schools in Hudson, Massachusetts. The Hudson school district won a National Schools of Character award from the Character Education Partnership in 2001, in part because of its strong service learning program. Berman believes so firmly in the value of CSL that he encourages teachers in his district to do projects yearly. CSL promotes civility in children, Berman believes, because it puts social responsibility into the curriculum, and it gets students to take action in a way that makes a difference to others.

In the best cases, students stay active and involved in their communities even after the CSL project ends. Or they apply skills learned during the project to other areas of their lives. In Denison, Iowa, a first-grade class regularly visited residents of the Alzheimer's Unit in a nearby nursing home. But many of the children didn't stop their involvement at the end of the school year. During the summer, they asked their families to take them to the nursing home for periodic visits. In Hudson, Massachusetts, one fourth grade teacher engaged her students in certifying a vernal pool, which is a way to protect a wetland area against development. The activity made such an impression on one student that he developed an enduring interest in protecting the environment. "What he did in fourth grade is still directing him," said his mother years later. As a middle schooler, for example, the student applied for and was accepted into a summer program for youths to study volcanoes in Hawaii. "Volcanoes in Hawaii, vernal pools in Massachusetts—it's all the same," says his fourth grade teacher Dawn Sather, acknowledging that, particulars aside, caring for the environment is an important thing to do.

CSL lets the community and young people see each other in a positive light.

Service learning can be an effective vehicle for changing negative perceptions and stereotypes. It lets the public see children as helpers, problem solvers, and people who care about their community. At the same time, CSL gives children an opportunity to know community members of different ages and backgrounds and to see that they are real people with real strengths, talents, needs, and wants. For example, when students from a Springfield, Massachusetts, middle school first visited a local nursing home to interview the residents for a biography project, many were scared that the senior citizens would be "mean" to them. But as the students spent time with the residents, they realized that the senior citizens were "nice" people, a lot like themselves. Meanwhile, the residents were impressed by how respectful the young people were and how thoroughly they had prepared for the interviews.

Additionally, service learning projects often generate positive media coverage, which lifts morale and fosters school and community pride. In North Adams, Massachusetts, the local newspaper published a story about children hosting a bus driver appreciation day as part of a larger bus bullying prevention project. In Leverett, Massachusetts, a radio station aired a segment about children helping to reintroduce salmon into their region's rivers. Such coverage lets a wider sphere of people know of the good work that students and community members are doing together and can spread feelings of appreciation and good will well beyond those who are actually involved in the project.

CSL allows those served and those serving to be both teachers and learners.

In good CSL, both the students and those they serve learn from each other and from the CSL experience. When a class of fifth graders in

Minneapolis became aware that first graders in their school could use help learning to read, they decided to make books on tape for the younger children. They also spent time listening to the tapes with the younger children and helping them follow along in the books. Although the fifth graders were the "teachers" in this project, it soon became clear that they were learning a lot from the first graders about nurturing.

CSL builds relationships between schools and community organizations.

When school children perform needed services in the community, support for the school grows. Community members and organizations become more involved in the school, and their support often develops into lasting relationships. In Springfield, Massachusetts, an elementary school has built a partnership with a hospital across the street. Hospital personnel and school children regularly move back and forth between the buildings for an array of health-related projects. And in Hudson, Massachusetts, fourth graders who wrote letters in support of the passage of a river protection act established a relationship with the state secretary of environmental affairs that has since grown into a lasting bond between the politician and the entire school. The secretary now returns regularly to the school to take part in environmental activities.

CSL re-energizes teachers and administrators.

In the Philadelphia school district, which has put in place a program to provide service learning activities for all of its 200,000 students, former superintendent David Hornbeck reported that "teachers say they feel inspired, creative, and passionate" when they use community service learning activities in their classrooms. Trust and cooperation grow as teachers and students become partners in learning. Todd Wallingford, a ninth grade civics teacher in Hudson, Massachusetts, and a strong advocate of service learning, says that "CSL is a great way to build a relationship with children."

Many teachers find that their stress level is reduced when students are engaged in service learning. When students are invested in learning and motivated to work, teachers see success for both the students and themselves. Also, teachers, who are traditionally isolated in their classroom, have opportunities through CSL to work with other adults in their schools and communities. Interacting with other teachers and school administrators, with personnel at various CSL sites, and often with experts or parent volunteers, teachers forge relationships, learn new things about their communities, and share conversations about their work—all of which can bring personal and professional growth.

Given these benefits, it's not surprising that community service learning tends to be catching. One class's involvement in a CSL project often inspires other classes in the school to join in or to do projects of their own. In North Adams, Massachusetts, the bus driver appreciation project gave another class in the school the idea to do a cafeteria worker appreciation day. In Hudson, Massachusetts, one class's wetlands projects led the entire grade in the school to launch similar efforts. Crossing state lines, a few classes' participation in restoring Atlantic salmon to the Connecticut River system has spread into a large regional effort involving schools in several Northeastern states. As action builds upon action and involvement leads to involvement, students, teachers, schools, and communities all benefit, and children learn important lessons about making their world a better place.

References:

Kielsmeier, James C. 2000. "A Time to Serve, A Time to Learn: Service-Learning and the Promise of Democracy," *Phi Delta Kappan* (May): 652–657.

Ratner, Nancy with Joan Schuman and Margaret Collins 1997. *Classrooms in the Community: Hampshire County Teachers Explore Community Service Learning.* Northampton, Massachusetts: Hampshire Educational Collaborative.

Types of Community Service Learning Projects

CSL projects can vary in structure, duration, and service theme. Here's a look at some of these variations and their benefits:

Project Structures

Single classroom

CSL projects most commonly involve a single classroom. The students may work together on the same project, all contributing toward the same goal, benefiting the same community, and most likely working at the same site. Or, they may split into small groups, each group working on a different project that fits into an overall theme. The latter was the case at Rochambeau Middle School in Connecticut, where students in a business enrichment class created their own businesses to raise money for various causes. Students formed small groups, each of which developed a different enterprise. They then pooled their earnings and decided as a class where to donate the money.

When all the students in a classroom work together on the same project, they can become a more cohesive community that appreciates the gifts of all classroom members. For example, CSL activities often put children in situations that require skills other than the day-to-day academic ones. This makes it possible for students who are not strong academically to take on leadership roles.

On the other hand, when the students break into small groups, the increased variety and choice may allow them to feel more invested in their work and learning. Working in small groups, they develop teamwork skills and, in many cases, learn how to work without continual adult supervision.

Two or more classrooms

In some cases, students from two or more classrooms work together on a CSL project, an arrangement that offers rich opportunities for learning. If the students are of different ages, the older students invariably take on the role of teacher and nurturer, while the younger children gain role models. Especially when there are opportunities for children from different grade levels to buddy up one on one, the older children learn from their "teacher" role and the younger children enjoy the attention of the big kids.

Sometimes, there is a very specific reason for two different grades to work together. For instance, a North Adams, Massachusetts, project to address bullying on the school bus began as a third grade project. But when the third graders noticed that many fifth graders, the oldest students in the school, were responsible for much of the bullying, they invited the older students to join the project and work on solving the problem together. This collaboration was one reason for the project's success.

Teachers also benefit when several classrooms are involved in CSL activities. Teachers can trade ideas and offer each other support. They can contribute their diverse talents, knowledge, and community connections in ways that strengthen the project and reduce each teacher's load.

Whole school

In whole-school projects, students can experience the power of many individuals working for a common goal. Any number of projects might be appropriate as whole-school endeavors: creating a community recycling center, designing and building an outdoor learning and exercise park, raising money to support arts education in the community, or putting on a bike-a-thon or walk-a-thon to bring visibility to a particular issue. These can all appeal to children of many different ages while easily allowing for connections to science, social studies, math, health, and other studies.

Whole-school projects repeated annually may also be a way to introduce younger children gradually to complex issues, particularly global issues. Trick-or-treating for UNICEF, a whole-school tradition at many American schools, can become a great opportunity for school-wide CSL. Most kindergartners and first graders cannot understand the causes of world poverty or conflict, or know the location of East Timor, Sudan, North Korea, or other possible beneficiaries of UNICEF aid. But they can learn that the money they collect helps some sick and hungry children in faraway places. At Greenfield Center School in Greenfield, Massachusetts, teachers link the UNICEF events to social studies, math, and other academic lessons geared to their students' abilities and curricular goals. Each year's learning builds on preceding years as children grapple with the issues at a level that's appropriate for their developmental stage. With increasing maturity, children are able to think beyond themselves and understand the issues more deeply.

Project Lengths

Projects completed within one year

CSL projects are almost always completed during one school year. However, within that time frame there are variations in length. For example, designing and planting a bulb garden on school grounds, a great way to use math and science skills, might take only a few weeks. But a senior citizen pen pal project might last all school year, while students learn and hone letter-writing skills over the course of months.

Short-term projects are a good starting point for teachers new to CSL. These projects are often more manageable than long-term projects and offer excellent opportunities for service and academic learning. On the other hand, the sustained activity of a long-term project can allow for greater service impact and depth of learning.

Some teachers repeat projects annually, establishing more and more links to the curriculum over the years. At a kindergarten center in Hudson, Massachusetts, each incoming class of kindergartners makes quilts for babies who live at a homeless shelter. Originally begun as part of learning the letter Q, the project has gained more language arts components each year, as well as math, science, and other academic tie-ins. Teachers have also incorporated lessons about families, safety, ethnicity, and creativity into the mix.

In addition, repeating projects can strengthen community ties. Ninth grade teacher Todd Wallingford reports that the first year his students approached community agencies about a CSL project, the agencies were skeptical. That changed when Wallingford kept doing projects year after year. "Now the agencies come to us," he says.

Multi-year projects

Sometimes it takes more than one school year to finish a CSL activity. Three of the Massachusetts projects profiled in this book are examples of this. In the dog poop project in Amherst, students ordered signs that would discourage dog owners from letting their pets leave droppings on the school playground. But the signs weren't finished and posted until the following year. In the Hudson vernal pool certification project, collecting and compiling the necessary data took three years, with each year's students continuing the previous class's work. And, in the North Adams bus bullying project, the project was carried over into a second year so that a bus driver appreciation piece could be added.

Although multi-year projects can be tricky to manage, the results can be worth the effort. During multi-year projects, children learn valuable lessons about achieving a long-term goal. They learn how to negotiate delays. They learn that important work takes time. And they learn that their work is part of a process, linked with past and future efforts.

Service Themes

Intergenerational

Some of the most popular CSL activities team students with senior citizens. These projects help young and old understand and appreciate each other. Intergenerational activities often involve students taking oral histories or writing biographies of the elderly. Students learn interviewing and writing skills and hear history told from a personal perspective. In return, they provide the seniors with companionship and a record of their life story. But even more importantly, such activities honor seniors' lives. Other CSL activities that serve senior citizens include helping with chores, hosting an intergenerational meal, or lobbying policy makers on behalf of an issue that affects the elderly.

Helping younger children

Even kindergartners can do projects that serve younger children, as illustrated by the quilt project in Hudson, Massachusetts. In that project, teachers helped students look beyond their own school for younger children who could benefit from a service learning project. Students can also look within their own school, asking "Is there something our class is studying that could be taught to younger students?" The answers can lead to CSL projects ranging from peer tutoring to performing student-written educational plays.

For example, at the K–8 Greenfield Center School in Greenfield, Massachusetts, seventh and eighth graders, who were studying industrialization and global labor issues, became concerned about labor practices in some countries, particularly child labor. As they researched the problem, they learned about ways they could help. They wanted to teach the younger grades some of what they learned. So they split up into small groups and gave presentations to every younger class, showing videos or doing role-plays that were appropriate for the age of the class. In addition, they organized an all-school fair to raise money for Rugmark and the Heifer Project, two organizations working to improve basic living and labor conditions around the world. For the fair, students got pledges from other students, parents, teachers, and staff for various "activity-thons"—shooting baskets at ten cents a basket or doing pushups at fifteen cents a pushup, for example. There were other games—guess the number of beans in the jar, fortune-telling, bowling—that students could play after paying a set entry fee. The fair raised $2,600. Equally important, the classroom presentation and the fair raised all grades' awareness of an important social issue and allowed the older and younger students to interact in a way that was mutually educational and nurturing.

Environmental

Environmental projects are suitable for students of all ages. Recycling drives and river cleanups are popular. Other efforts include campaigning for the protection of a wetland or other ecologically important area, making and selling bird houses with the proceeds going to an environmental organization, developing and maintaining nature trails, planting trees, or painting a mural depicting local flora and fauna. Environmental activities can also connect to a wide range of curriculum areas, including science, math, language arts, social studies, art, and physical education.

Humanitarian

Projects that address issues of hunger and poverty, homelessness, and social injustice fall into this category. Children might organize a community meal, collect food for a food pantry or clothing for a homeless shelter, or work with an organization such as Habitat for Humanity to build or renovate a house. Combining this kind of service with curriculum lessons allows students to gain some understanding of the causes of poverty and other social problems. Academic tasks such as researching and graphing data on hunger or planning budgets for various income levels can make the abstract notions more concrete and personal.

In projects that provide direct assistance, it's important to get input from the communities served. When those benefiting from the service help shape the project, they become partners with the students rather than simply being recipients of a handout, which can feel demeaning. One teacher described her class's experience with a book drive for a resource-poor school. The students doing the project had a lengthy and warm correspondence with the students who would receive the books. The children told each other about their daily activities, exchanged small gifts, and discussed the book project. Because of the mutual respect and understanding that developed, the recipients were extremely pleased when the books were presented.

Health and safety

Projects that address health and safety issues will vary depending on students' age as well as community need. Younger students, for example, may be more interested in activities that focus on bike safety or fire prevention. Older students might want to examine issues of harassment in their school. There are lots of other possibilities: In areas where crime is a significant concern, a CSL project on crime prevention may be valuable. If a neighborhood park is close to a dangerous intersection, students might address traffic safety. In places where wildlife is plentiful, students might educate the public on the dangers of rabies to humans and pets.

Animals

Most children enjoy any project that helps animals. Many animal shelters welcome young children to play with or groom the animals, make toys for them, or raise money or do publicity for the shelter. Children can also help out at a wildlife refuge, adopt a whale, educate others about an endangered species, visit with sick animals at a veterinary clinic, or contribute to biodiversity studies by helping to identify and count local species.

Public policy

In all of the above service areas, there are opportunities for projects that try to inform relevant public policies or persuade the public to take political action. These projects generally work best with older elementary or middle school students. Voter registration drives fall into this category and may fit nicely with a study of the U. S. electoral process. Conducting a letter writing campaign, gathering signatures on a petition, writing public service announcements and getting them aired are examples of activities that can help influence public policy while enhancing academic learning. Although teachers should be aware of how such activities might be received by parents and the community, especially if the issue involved is controversial, they should not automatically avoid sensitive topics. In fact, students can learn valuable lessons from taking a stand, however unpopular. But, teachers need to gauge the community's feelings, weigh the potential risks to students, and prepare them for the range of possible reactions.

Steps in Doing a Community Service Learning Project

There are five basic steps in implementing a CSL project:

1. Deciding on a project

2. Planning the logistics

3. Doing the activities

4. Reflecting on the experience

5. Celebrating and sharing the project with others

When children are involved in all of these steps—not just step three—the project becomes much more meaningful.

Deciding on a Project

There are two main ways to decide on a project: Start with the curriculum and look for service opportunities related to it, or start with a service that students could provide and connect it to academic learning.

Starting with the curriculum

Any academic subject can be the starting point for a CSL project. The key is to look for service activities that let students expand on academic learning. If the class is studying aquatic animals, could they hook up with local naturalists to help protect the wildlife of the area's rivers and lakes? If health and nutrition is a curriculum emphasis, could students raise money and awareness about hunger and poverty in their community? If children are learning measurement and fractions, could they plan and build a garden for a community center?

Starting with community service

A CSL project might emerge from classroom conversations about school or community needs and problems. When the third grade class in North Adams, Massachusetts, discussed bullying on their school buses, a problem at many schools across the country, the students enthusiastically decided to do a CSL project that focused on improving bus behavior. Their high energy and creativity continued throughout the project. If the local library is in need of newer books, discussing it with students might lead to a student-organized book drive. Students' awareness of local river pollution might result in their organizing river cleanup efforts. "If you tap into the right community need, the project just takes off," says CSL proponent Todd Wallingford.

Some CSL projects derive from students' responses to a local emergency or from their concerns over national or international disasters they have heard about in the media. Often these projects spring up unplanned. For instance, when six firefighters died while fighting a fire in Worcester, Massachusetts, in 1999, a couple of fourth graders in nearby Hudson started collecting money at lunchtime for the grieving families. When their teacher gave an assignment to the whole class to write a news report about the disaster, the spontaneous money collection, now tied to the curriculum, became the seed for a CSL project. The students used math and language arts skills as they raised money, wrote letters, and planned several events, including a picnic for the firefighters at the end of the year. The more the children learned, the more involved they became. And, in addition to academic benefits, the children developed meaningful relationships with local firefighters.

Teachers can reinforce several curriculum areas through a single project, no matter whether the project started with the curriculum or with service. For example, second graders at one California school grow vegetables to contribute to a local food co-op. The project teaches many math and science concepts. But the teacher also ties the project to social studies, asking children why there's a need for a co-op in addition to nearby supermarkets. She reinforces language arts by having children make posters and ads about their vegetables, and teaches Spanish by having children learn the Spanish names of the vegetables.

It's important to make sure the project suits children's age and experience. To gauge if a project is appropriate, see if students can answer the following questions: What is the problem we're trying to address? Whom will we help? How will we help them? The depth with which children can think about these questions varies with developmental level, but if they're going to benefit from doing a CSL project, they need to be able to consider the questions. If two grades are working together on CSL, the project should appeal to both age groups and there should be ways for both age groups to contribute. (See the box, "Consider Children's Developmental Level," page 22, for more.)

It's also important to offer students some choices. Middle school students at a school in Indiana choose among half a dozen service sites around their city, signing up for the site that interests them the most. A seventh grade business-focused enrichment class in Connecticut decides both what kind of businesses to create for their CSL project and who will receive their proceeds. Children taking part in the Heifer Project at a New Hampshire school decide where to send their aid. Allowing children to make some choices helps them become more invested in their work. When children make choices, they practice taking initiative and being creative. And they tend to set appropriate challenges for themselves so that they get the most out of their experience.

Consider Children's Developmental Level

For a CSL project to be effective, the community served and the problem addressed need to be tailored to children's developmental level. Children younger than seven are most likely to understand concepts about the here and now—the things and people they see in their immediate environment. At around age seven, children begin to grasp the idea of long ago and far away and are more able to use symbols, tools, and imagination to understand places, people, and events they can't see. Their ability to grasp abstract ideas then continues to grow incrementally at ages nine, ten, and up.

One way to apply this knowledge of child development to designing CSL projects, says Chip Wood, co-founder of Northeast Foundation for Children, is to picture a series of concentric circles. The innermost circle represents communities closest to the children: their class and their school. The next circle represents the children's neighborhood. The third circle represents the town and state, and so on.

As children age, their focus widens out from the innermost circle to encompass more and more circles. Thus, kindergartners would get the most out of CSL projects that help their classroom or school. Although activities to improve their school will continue to hold interest for students in second and third grade, projects to help their neighborhood might also be appropriate. From fourth grade on, activities benefiting students' town and beyond may be suitable. Middle schoolers especially love to go outside of school and work on projects that help the environment, such as recycling drives or river cleanups.

Developmental considerations should come into play when deciding on the type of issue to address as well. "Issues can't be simply an adult agenda imposed on kids," says Hudson, Massachusetts, superintendent Sheldon Berman. Good CSL projects, like good teaching, capture children where they really live, meshing with the child's needs and interests at the moment.

Looking at CSL through the developmental lens reveals why the dog poop project, the school playground project described in the section "Five Projects In-Depth," was so appropriate for first graders, explains Joan Cenedella, education consultant and former vice president for academic affairs at Bank Street College of Education. The children did something to help their school, a community that they could easily grasp, and they addressed an issue of keen interest to them. Nine-year-olds might have said, "Eewww!" to dog poop and scoffed at doing a project on it, says Cenedella. But, as teachers and parents the world over know, first graders deal in the concrete. They're interested in what they can see and in how things work. Fascinated by bodily functions, children this age were naturally captivated by making their playground safe from pet droppings.

Planning the Logistics

Once the teacher and students have chosen a project, they can begin planning. This happens at two levels: teacher-only planning and teacher-student planning.

Planning by the teacher

Before inviting students' input, the teacher should investigate the feasibility and scope of the project. This helps keep the project from feeling overwhelming to students. Questions to ask include the following:

- How much time will this project take? How much time can we devote?
- When will the service take place? What part of the day? When during the school year?
- Are there any transportation needs, and how will they be met?
- Are there any expenses, and how will they be covered?
- How and when will students reflect on the project?
- How will we assess students' work?

Planning with students

Students can make valuable contributions to project planning. Here are some questions that may be appropriate to discuss with students, depending on their age:

- Is this something our class can handle alone, or do we need to get other students involved?
- Should students form small groups, each working on one part of the project?
- How can we get support from parents, the school, and the larger community?

- How will we celebrate our project and share with others what we learned?

Some issues, of course, straddle the two levels of planning. For example, questions about transportation and expenses can benefit from student input after the teacher has done some preliminary thinking. If money needs to be raised, students can help plan fund-raisers. If transportation is a problem, students may have ideas for modifying the project so that activities can be done within walking distance of the school.

It's okay to start small. Teachers often continue a CSL project from one year to the next, expanding their scope as more sources of support are identified and more community connections emerge.

Doing the Activities

Careful planning can make a big difference in how smoothly the project goes. But even with the best planning, there will be many moments when teachers will need to steer, manage, correct, nudge, and boost. Here are some points to keep in mind:

Students might need to learn how to perform some of the tasks.

CSL projects often involve a range of tasks, from making phone calls to hammering nails, that students might not know how to do. They need to be taught and given time to practice. For example, it might be helpful to list the steps in making phone calls: How do we introduce ourselves when we call an organization? How do we ask for the right person to speak to? How do we quickly explain what we need? How do we thank the person at the end of the conversation? Students could write a script and then, in pairs, rehearse making the calls.

Students need to learn how to behave in unfamiliar settings.

Preparing students for unfamiliar settings and teaching them appropriate behavior is just as important as teaching needed skills. Before first graders in Iowa visited the Alzheimer's unit of a local nursing home, the teacher carefully explained Alzheimer's disease and its effect on people. She told students that residents might repeat questions many times. She suggested appropriate topics of conversation and taught children what to do if the residents didn't respond. Once at the nursing home, the children were respectful and calm in their interactions with residents, an outcome that the teacher attributes in large part to the careful classroom preparation. Even when students go to settings that may seem fairly commonplace—an office, a park, another school, a college—it's always helpful to spend time on preparation.

Break up long projects.

Breaking up a long project into chunks, each with its own clear finish line, can give children a sense of progress along the way. In a garden project, planting the seeds and growing the seedlings might be one chunk, building the raised flower beds might be another, transplanting and watering may be the next, and harvesting and distributing the vegetables might be the last chunk. Clearly acknowledging the completion of each phase, perhaps with a mini-celebration, can help children stay involved in the project.

Mistakes are opportunities to improve the project.

Mistakes can and do happen in the course of a CSL project. Children—and teachers—need to know that it's okay to make mistakes, but it's also important to do something about them. Handled responsibly, mistakes can lead to greater learning and to improvements in the project. For example, when an understandable oversight in the North Adams, Massachusetts, bus bullying project caused some bus drivers to feel blamed for children's misbehavior, the teachers decided to extend the project for another year. The teachers believed that misbehavior on the bus would decrease if children had meaningful relationships with the drivers. So, in the second year, the children got to know the drivers and learned about the demands of their job. In this case, addressing a mistake resulted in a much more effective project.

Reflecting on the Experience

Teachers who lead successful CSL projects incorporate regular opportunities for reflection. They recognize that children learn more effectively if they have time to think, talk, and write about their experiences. As Rahima Wade says, teachers can best facilitate reflection by cultivating a calm and unhurried environment where children feel safe to express their views. (Wade 1997, 71) Teachers prompt students to think about and discuss what they've learned, what has surprised them, what has worked well, what problems they've encountered, what has helped them solve the problems, and why their project has been important.

Here are some things to remember about reflection:

Reflection can help dispel stereotypes.

In the world of CSL, children often interact with people outside their small school circle. These encounters with unfamiliar people and places may bring up—and challenge—stereotypes. Taking time for reflection helps students understand and work through their reactions. For example, in the biography writing project in Springfield, Massachusetts, class discussions were instrumental in helping students sort out their changed perceptions of the elderly. Slowing down to think and talk helped the students develop empathy. In his book *Time to Teach, Time to Learn,* Chip Wood advocates reflection throughout the school day, writing, "It's hard to put yourself

in someone else's shoes when your shoes are always on the run."
(Wood 1999, 271)

Reflection takes many forms.

Keeping a personal journal or learning log is a popular and valuable method of reflection. But there are other methods, too, including partner chats; small group discussions; short written musings exchanged with a partner; letters to a pen pal; and artistic expression such as poems, essays, music, dance, and drawings or other artwork.

Reflection should be ongoing.

A one-time wrap-up discussion at the end of a project can give children a sense of closure. But ongoing reflection helps children cultivate the habit of thoughtfulness. Regular reflection doesn't have to use lots of class time. At the end of a week's work, students can take twenty minutes to write in their journals. Or in a project where two classrooms collaborate, students can gather for brief discussions after each work session. Reflection periods can take place whenever students seem ready, just so long as they take place and take place often.

Celebrating and Sharing the Project with Others

Celebration and sharing take the reflection process one step further. As students invite recognition for their accomplishments, they encounter new questions, make new connections, and extend their learning.

Celebrating

Celebrations of CSL projects run the gamut from formal receptions away from school to casual gatherings in the children's own class-room. Sometimes lots of people are invited—all those connected to the project, the rest of the school, community leaders, parents, and administrators. Other times only the students and a small core of closely involved people attend.

Sharing

Students' sharing, which often takes place during the celebration, can take various forms. In the most basic kind of sharing, students describe their project and show any resulting product—for example, a pamphlet, a quilt, a fleece hat. But students may also enjoy stretching their creativity. Students who did a voter registration project might produce a play or video to represent their experience. A class that helped construct a nature trail might create a mural that depicts the various strands of their learning. A class that raised money for a homeless shelter might write a group poem or collection of stories that captures their insights and feelings about homelessness. These sorts of representations ask students to synthesize what they learned, deepening the learning even more.

In addition to reinforcing children's learning and boosting their self-worth, the celebration and sharing of CSL projects can rally support from parents and the public. And celebrations, which might get media attention, can broaden the impact of the CSL activity by inspiring others to serve.

References:

Wade, Rahima C., editor. 1997. *Community Service Learning: A Guide to Including Service in the Public School Curriculum.* Albany, New York: SUNY Press.

Wood, Chip. 1999. *Time to Teach, Time to Learn: Changing the Pace of School.* Greenfield, Massachusetts: Northeast Foundation for Children.

Attributes of Effective
CSL Projects

- They are part of the academic curriculum. They reinforce or expand students' academic skills.

- They provide a genuinely needed community service. The service effectively addresses a problem rather than merely allowing students to feel good.

- They are geared to students' developmental level. Both the community served and the issues addressed are ones children can grasp, given their age and experience.

- They offer students some choice. Students help decide on a project and have a role in planning its details.

- They allow time for students to learn needed knowledge or skills. Teachers take the time to teach the skills needed for the project and the behaviors appropriate for the settings where students will be working.

- They include opportunities for ongoing reflection. Students are encouraged to think and talk about their experiences throughout the project.

- They end with some sort of celebration and sharing. Students celebrate their work.

Questions
and Concerns

1. What if I have a service idea, but I don't know who might benefit?

Many teachers find themselves in this situation. They know that a quilt making or biography writing project would be great for their class, but they don't know who should receive the quilts or whose biographies to write. Or they feel that testing the local water supply would be a valuable activity, but they don't know which local officials to approach.

Start by describing your idea to friends, other teachers, and parents. Someone may have information about an appropriate agency or have helpful connections in the service world. Read your local newspaper for ideas. Check the front of your phone book for listings of area service agencies and contact organizations in your school's neighborhood.

For large-scale service projects, a more formal process might be necessary. Ed Kaufman, a teacher in Acton, Massachusetts, organizes an annual multi-site CSL project for 100 fifth and sixth graders. When he started the project, he formed a Site Development Committee of ten parents and one teacher. The committee generated a list of possible sites and developed a set of questions to ask each site. The questions, which helped the committee evaluate the appropriateness of the site, covered issues such as site safety, staff interest in working with children, and availability of an on-site coordinator.

2. How do I find the time to organize CSL projects?

Organizing a CSL project can take time. Most teachers agree, however, that the rewards are more than worth any extra time invested. Nancy Gallagher, adjustment counselor at Brayton Elementary School in North Adams, Massachusetts, co-led the school's bus bullying CSL project. She advises teachers to start small as a way to minimize the organizing time. "You don't have to do everything in one project," she says. Gallagher also recommends finding a partner, perhaps another teacher, who can share the workload. If your school or district has a CSL coordinator, make full use of his/her help. Finally, make sure that the CSL activity is solidly connected to curriculum goals, not an add-on, so that it deserves the time you put into it.

3. What if I'm already doing service projects and want to turn them into CSL projects?

Great! Just look at your curriculum to see where you can make connections. Start with math and language arts. If you're already collecting food for a food pantry, for example, maybe students can research how many people use the food pantry and do some graphing. Or, perhaps they can write letters to the editor of a local newspaper describing what they've learned and asking the public for donations.

Don't forget to add time for structured reflection. As Massachusetts teacher Todd Wallingford points out, "If reflection is not done with guidance and in a structured way, students might walk away with some of their biases reinforced rather than struck down."

4. How much funding do CSL projects usually require, and how might I get that funding?

Most projects require relatively little money, especially if the service activity takes place within the school. For projects that involve activities away from school, the most common expenses are transportation and extra-curriculum materials. (See question 5 for more about transportation.)

The federal government provides funding for CSL projects through each state department of education. In addition, many state governments and school districts offer their own mini-grants. These often include a stipend for the teacher. Contact your district office or your state department of education to find out about all these sources of support.

Many teachers get funding from local businesses, regional offices of large corporations, and service organizations such as Rotary Club or Lions Club. Businesses may be willing to provide in-kind services if they don't want to make a cash donation. For example, a grocery store might donate food, and a printer might donate printing services. Pitch your idea, and if some groups turn you down, don't take it as a sign that the community isn't willing to support your project. Keep trying. Support is out there—it's a matter of finding the right group.

See the "Community Service Learning Resources" section at the end of this book for organizations that may be helpful.

5. How can I provide transportation to service sites?

You may be able to hire a bus, perhaps with funding from the sources mentioned in question 4, or a bus company may donate its services. Many teachers find that parents are happy to drive if they can. Often one parent or a small committee organizes parent drivers.

Don't forget that there may be good opportunities for service learning right on your own school grounds or within walking distance. In fact, most of the projects profiled in this book fit this description. From reading to the school's younger children to visiting residents at a nearby nursing home, there are numerous possibilities for CSL projects that require no transportation.

ɔ. How can I get more support from parents and school administrators?

First of all, be assured that there is strong support for CSL among parents and the general public. In 2000, the W. K. Kellogg Foundation and the Ewing Marion Kauffman Foundation had a poll done of 1,000 Americans, half of whom were parents of school-age children. When given a definition of CSL, ninety percent of the respondents said they would support it in their local public schools. The overwhelming majority agreed that CSL improves students' grasp of academic basics and helps students build skills needed for later success in life. (Academy for Educational Development)

That said, teachers often need to help parents understand CSL and to rally support among parents and administrators. Todd Wallingford says the best way to gain support is to offer testimonials from the children. "Whenever you make presentations, you've got to have the kids speak. Kids are the best spokespeople for CSL." Wallingford recommends making presentations to the school board as well as inviting school board members, parents, administrators, and the community to an open house where children speak. The children's knowledge and excitement about what they've learned will be infectious. Remember, however, to have students prepare and practice carefully for such presentations so they will communicate their enthusiasm successfully. Articles in the newspaper and students' letters to the editor also can help build community support.

Sheldon Berman, superintendent of the Hudson, Massachusetts, school district, suggests referring administrators to the Compact for Learning and Citizenship, which is dedicated to linking CSL to the curriculum. See "Community Service Learning Resources" at the end of this book for contact information.

7. I'm under tremendous pressure to meet academic standards. Is there any evidence that CSL improves academics?

Research about CSL is still in its early stages and is mostly anecdotal or derived from individual CSL program evaluations. Still, this early evidence is very encouraging. In an article in the May 2000 issue of *Phi Delta Kappan,* Shelley Billig, vice president of RMC Research Corporation in Denver, summarizes a number of research articles that support the academic benefits of CSL. For example, in Springfield, Massachusetts, participation in CSL was associated with higher scores in the state's basic skills test, and in Indiana, students who took part in CSL had higher standardized test scores on Indiana's state assessment in third and eighth grade math and English than students who didn't participate. Also, in several middle schools across the country, students who participated in service-learning tutoring programs improved their grades and test scores in language arts and math. Other studies, too, have had similar findings. (Billig 2000)

8. How can I assess children's participation in CSL activities?

Many educators, including Chip Wood, co-founder of Northeast Foundation for Children, say that while CSL may require different assessment methods than those used to assess more traditional student work, assessment is possible because CSL is performance-based. Wood suggests that before the project begins, teachers should establish a rubric that sets out what kind of performance is considered minimally satisfactory, what kind is considered reasonable, and what kind is considered exemplary.

Teachers can also use rubrics to assess service activities. At the Discovery School in Richmond, Indiana, sixth through eighth graders taking part in CSL serve at various sites around the city. The assessment rubric for their service covers four areas: communication with the service site supervisor, commitment to the service job, quality of work completed, and dependability. Based on various kinds of information, including responses from site supervisors and the teachers' observations, students receive one of four "grades" in each performance area. The grades are denoted by the words "developing," "confident," "fluent," and "mastery." For example, in the area of dependability, students who need reminders to keep working get a grade of "developing." Those who stay focused on the job ninety percent of the time get a grade of "confident." Students who work hard all the time are "fluent." And being a leader in their service group and encouraging others to stay on task earns students the assessment of "mastery."

Many teachers invite students to evaluate their own performance—on the academic assignments, the service activities, or both. Students might use the rubrics established for the project along with check-lists and guided journal reflections to arrive at conclusions about their own performance. Engaging students in self-evaluations like this can enhance students' self-awareness, encourage responsibility, help students set goals, and make them more invested in their learning.

References:

Academy for Educational Development. "Service-learning Delivers What Americans Want from Schools." Web article from www.learningindeed.org. Accessed September 2000.

Billig, Shelley. 2000. "Research on K–12 School-based Service-Learning: The Evidence Builds." *Phi Delta Kappan.* (May): 658-664.

Five Projects
In-Depth

The Dog Poop Project

School: Crocker Farm Elementary School,
Amherst, Massachusetts

Grade level: first

Demographics: grades K–6, 300 students,
semi-rural college town

Academic areas emphasized: health,
language arts, math, science, social studies

Service theme: health and safety

Project Summary

The twenty-two students in Jan Demers's first grade class became
fed up with stepping in dog poop on the playground. To tackle this
problem, the children brainstormed ideas about how to clean up

their playground, drew up an action plan, and formed committees. Some children researched the health issues of dog feces; others called town officials to research relevant laws.

The next step was to document the problem. To do this, the children formed a "poop patrol," using their recess time to take Polaroid photos of dog piles. They then wanted to tell the community about the problem. The children designed signs reminding people to clean up after their dogs and had the signs made with funds from a CSL grant. They wrote letters to the local newspaper and contacted a local TV station, which did a story for the evening news.

The project was hugely successful. Five years later, there continues to be less dog poop on the playground. The students, who are currently sixth graders, still feel a sense of ownership of the project and the playground. They occasionally stop by to report "infractions" to their former first grade teacher, who often gets similar reports from other students in the school.

The project's success derived from its clear and concrete connection to the children's lives. Because the subject matter and the community served were easy for the children to understand, the project was ideally suited to the children's age and developmental stage.

On a project like this, the curriculum tie-ins are many. There are health lessons about germs carried by dog feces and science lessons about the digestive system. Civics lessons result from contacting local officials about laws and the rights of dog owners. In the area of language arts, students learn communication through writing letters, speaking on the phone, contacting the media, and making signs. Math projects can revolve around dog census information.

Most important for the Crocker Farm children was learning how to be a citizen in a democracy. As one of them told a reporter at the time, "I learned that we can make a difference if we take a stand."

> A good CSL project for younger children involves a
> community need that has direct relevance to their lives—
> for instance, a problem that affects their living and learning
> in the school community—and results in something tangible,
> so they can see evidence of what they've done.

Jan Demers, first grade teacher
Crocker Farm Elementary School
Amherst, Massachusetts

Project Description

Jan Demers is sitting in her classroom after school at Crocker Farm
Elementary, a neighborhood school in Amherst, Massachusetts. She
is reminiscing with three of her former students about the community service learning project they did in her class five years ago.
Crammed into tiny chairs, the sixth grade girls still have vivid memories of their first grade effort to make the school playground clean.

"I remember it all started when somebody stepped in dog poop on
the playground and tracked it in on the rug. We were all saying
'What's that smell?'," recalls one of the girls.

Demers knew that playground cleanup would be a great CSL project
for her first graders. "This project had a direct connection to
children's lives," she says, "because every youngster has stepped in
dog poop." Demers, now in her twenty-sixth year of teaching, also
knew that six-year-olds, interested in bodily functions, would be
naturally interested in poop, even if a little self-conscious about it.
One of the sixth grade girls concurs, "Now we'd say 'That's dis-
gusting! We don't want to do that!'." But back then, poop was a
suitable topic of conversation. And cleaning up poop on the playground served a community—the school—that the young children
could easily grasp.

On a day in May not long after the rug-tracking incident, Demers
introduced the project to her inclusive classroom of twenty-two

youngsters. Together they read the book *Everyone Poops* by Taro Gomi. This straightforward and humorous book helped the class work through its initial response of embarrassed giggles and develop a way of talking about the problem.

At that first meeting, the class discussed why dog poop on the playground was a problem and who was responsible for solving it. Demers told the children that they could have a hand in finding a solution.

"We looked at it in terms of the whole school community," Demers says. She helped the children see that this project, which arose from their own experiences, would also serve others because it would benefit the entire school.

They brainstormed ideas for solving the dog poop problem and Demers created a web of issues on the chart board: Are there laws? Does dog poop have germs? Should we ask a vet, a dogcatcher, a nurse?

Four committees and a poop patrol

The next day they drew up an action plan. Using the phone directory, they determined which town services might be helpful. They discussed what other resources were available—for example, the school nurse, their parents, and their neighbors.

Then they formed four committees—Health, Dog Information, Law, and Spread the News—and children signed up according to their interests. The children learned that committees were a way for a large group of people to organize and share the workload. Each committee had one or two tasks to complete.

The Law group rehearsed making phone calls, then went to the school office to phone town hall with the help of a parent. The children discovered that there was no "pooper scooper" law in Amherst.

With the help of another parent, who worked at the School of Public Health at nearby University of Massachusetts, the children on the Health Committee examined a book that gave information about roundworms and other health hazards of dog feces.

"I remember that book," says one of the sixth grade girls about the text, *Animal Agents and Vectors of Human Disease*, by Paul C. Beaver and Rodney C. Jung. "It was a really big book. I remember thinking that we were studying something really serious."

Demers helped her students find the appropriate information in the text, and the proficient readers in the class read a passage to the others. One quote in particular stood out because it used words that were key to the first graders' problem: "dogs" and "playgrounds." It answered their question "How do we know it's not healthy to have dog poop on the playground?" and enabled the students to speak with authority about the situation.

During all this time, an ongoing activity was the "poop patrol." Children organized themselves into groups and, at recess, roamed the playground looking for evidence to support their concerns. The children photographed their findings, using a Polaroid camera that Demers bought with part of a $300 CSL grant from the Hampshire Educational Collaborative, a local community agency.

"It was a big thrill to take pictures," says one of the sixth graders. "Someone would say 'dog poop under the pine trees!' and we'd all run down there to photograph it." "I remember everybody wanted to take pictures," says another, recalling how much fun they had integrating the project into their play at recess and how other classes informally joined in.

Making the news

Once the children had documented the problem and gained some understanding of the health hazards, they wanted to communicate their concerns to others. They wrote practice letters to the editor of their local newspaper. Compiling the best of the letters into one, the class sent it to the *Amherst Bulletin*, which published it. In their letter, the class quoted from *Animal Agents and Vectors of Human Disease* and then wrote, "Please make a law so that people will have to clean up after their dogs. We don't want to get germs and get sick!"

The Spread the News committee also phoned area television stations. A child would initiate the call, then Demers would step in to further explain the situation. One station sent a crew to the school to interview the children and ran a story on the local evening news called "Canine Landmines."

The children decided to use the remaining money from the grant to put up signs around the school grounds, reminding people that the playground was not a dog's bathroom. A group looked in the Yellow Pages for the names of sign companies and chose the one that, on the phone, sounded the most interested in working with them. After poring over the examples of pre-made signs, the children voted to create their own. The design they came up with showed a dog's face with the words: "Dog poop can spread disease. Please pick up after your dog." They ordered three signs and posted one at the entrance to the playground, one by the driveway to the school, and one on a footpath frequented by dog walkers.

On a day near the end of school, the children reflected on their learning experience in this very hands-on, child-directed project. Reflecting with first graders mostly involves helping them realize how they feel and giving them labels for their feelings, says Demers. She told her students, "Another name for that kind of happiness you feel when you've worked hard on a project is 'pride.'"

In their discussion, the children also revealed a real knowledge of the related academic areas and an understanding of how to work together to solve a problem. They could talk about the health hazards of dog feces and demonstrate a rudimentary knowledge about town government. They learned how to write letters and experienced a

Special Considerations in Working with Young Children

"Don't feel that because the students are young they can't do a community service learning project," says Jan Demers. "They might need help reading or writing, but the ideas are their own."

Here are some things to remember when doing CSL with early elementary children:

1. When choosing a project, consider issues that children themselves might bring up, such as things that affect their daily school lives. Be careful not to impose adult agendas on children.

2. Keep the project small and at a level that the children can understand. Generally, the community served should be the classroom, school, or neighborhood.

3. Make sure the project will bring tangible results.

4. Children this age are not capable of deep reflection, though some kind of simple reflection, such as identifying feelings, is important.

5. Getting grants for projects with this age group is possible, even though grant questions usually seem geared towards older students. Don't be intimidated!

behind-the-scenes glimpse of television, comparing their experience of being interviewed for TV with the final edited piece on the news.

Demers noticed that her students felt empowered as they took on the task of solving the dog poop problem. She saw them working well with each other and with adults as they searched for the solution. Children commented that they liked working in a group and helping their community. One student said she learned that even small children can do something important.

A teacher's reflections

The Dog Poop Project was Demers's first experience with community service learning. Looking back, would she have done anything differently? Demers says she would have started the project earlier, because "things happen very slowly." When the class's letter to the editor was published, school was already out for the summer. And, getting the signs made took so much time that the students weren't able to see them posted until the next year.

Academically, Demers would add a math piece. For example, she would have the children undertake a dog census to determine how many dogs live in the neighborhoods around the school and then have the children make graphs from that data. But, in spite of these concerns, she thought the project was so successful that she now does a CSL project every year.

Life-changing lessons

One sign of the project's success is the way it became deeply integrated into the children's lives. Organizing themselves into the Poop Patrol at recess, writing "Odes to Dog Poop" during a poetry unit, and continuing to notice the condition of the playground year after year, these students experienced learning in a way that was relevant and empowering. And, although the town has not enacted any laws requiring owners to pick up after their dogs, the signs are still up at the school and the playground is much cleaner.

"Addressing this problem was important," Demers says. "These are children growing up in a democratic society and hopefully they'll become proactive in their communities."

To judge from the conversation with the sixth grade girls who have dropped by her classroom, being proactive is a lesson well learned. When Demers mentions that her current kindergarten class is going to tackle the problem of broken swings on the playground, the sixth graders are immediately interested and full of ideas, from surveys to fund-raisers to posters. As Demers piles the chairs on top of the table, the girls hatch plans to work with her class on this new CSL project.

Demers wonders if they know how to jump into action so quickly because of their experience as first graders, solving the dog poop problem. Listening to the girls' discussion as she turns out the lights, she smiles. She likes to think so.

Resource used by Jan Demers:

Gomi, Taro. 1993. *Everyone Poops.* Translated by Amanda Mayer Stinchecum. Brooklyn, New York: Kane/Miller Book Publishers.

The Bus Bully Project

School: Brayton Elementary School,
North Adams, Massachusetts

Grade levels: third and fifth

Demographics: grades pre-K–5,
500-plus students, small city

Academic areas emphasized:
language arts, science

Service themes: helping younger
children, health and safety

Project Summary

Frustration over bullying on the school bus led to two years of community service learning projects for third and fifth graders at Brayton

Elementary School. Brayton Elementary is a pre-K–5 school in North Adams, Massachusetts, the smallest city in Massachusetts.

In the first year of the project, Karen Lefave's third grade class enlisted the help of fifth graders, the oldest students in the school, to find a solution to the fighting and name calling that permeated the school bus ride.

After discussing the inappropriate behavior and jotting down each incident in their notebooks, the students decided to focus on bullying—how it feels to be bullied, what might cause someone to bully others, and how to respond to this behavior. They brainstormed ways to address the problem, drew pictures and wrote stories about their worries, role-played, kept journals, and took surveys before and after the project. At the end of the year, they invited bus drivers and school and town officials to a "bullyproofing presentation."

The next year, the students brought the bus drivers into the project. The students knew that children behave better in the classroom because they have a relationship with their teachers. Wouldn't bus behavior improve if students got to know the bus drivers? Working in mixed third–fifth grade groups, the children interviewed the eight school bus drivers, took their photos, made posters, and organized "Bus Driver Appreciation Day" for the whole school.

Still in these working groups, the students also took a look at the bus rules. Realizing that the language of the rules was difficult to understand, they rewrote the rules in kid-friendly language and distributed them to the rest of the school.

In addition to learning they could make a difference, students used a range of academic skills. In the course of the project, they wrote in their journals, shared entries, wrote letters, composed short skits for role-playing activities, created a brochure of bus rules, and spoke in front of an audience—all of which called on language arts skills. In identifying and recording bullying behavior, they learned the process of scientific inquiry and observation. Throughout the project, they practiced the important social skills of active listening, empathy, and assertion.

Assessments showed positive results: After the project's first year, behavior incidents reported by bus drivers were cut in half. Noting that the projects empowered both her students and herself, Lefave said that her students became young social activists ready to tackle a long list of projects. And, inspired by the project's success, another class in the school organized a day of appreciation for cafeteria workers.

[The students'] feelings were validated. And, it was empowering for myself as well. It reminded me that there's more to school than academics. There are emotional and physical safety issues going on, too.

Karen Lefave, third grade teacher
Brayton Elementary School
North Adams, Massachusetts

Project Description

"There is not a school system in the world that doesn't have a bus problem," says Deb Coyne, service learning coordinator for schools in North Adams, Massachusetts. "But since it is not an easy fix," she continues, "you don't talk about it."

Coyne was teaching a course on community service learning pedagogy for pre-K–12 teachers when a member of the course, third grade teacher Karen Lefave, had what Coyne describes as an "ah-ha moment." Lefave realized that bullying on the school bus, one of the most painful problems her students faced, could be addressed as a community service learning project.

Lefave, now in her twenty-third year as a teacher in North Adams schools, had become increasingly concerned about how the morning

49

bus ride affected her students. "The bullying set the tone for the whole day and often left my third graders in tears," she says. She also saw her students dawdling at the end of the day, trying to avoid riding the bus back home.

Lefave approached school adjustment counselor Nancy Gallagher. Gallagher, too, was frustrated with trying to address the school bus problem. As part of her preventive work in the classrooms, Gallagher had tried group meetings that were focused on the school bus problem, but they had not been as helpful as she wanted.

The two realized that bus misbehavior was a huge problem. Making any significant improvement would require action by students, teachers, bus drivers, parents, and administrators. But they also knew they didn't need to fix all of it at once. To start, they would focus on helping students recognize and effectively respond to bullying— in themselves and others.

A project is born

They began talking about bus concerns with the students in Lefave's inclusive classroom. Children could easily identify the inappropriate behavior—the swearing, yelling, pushing, and general chaos that typified the bus ride. When Lefave asked if they wanted to do something about it, they eagerly agreed.

She told them that first they had to be scientists and make observations. In journals, they jotted down incidents that they witnessed on the school bus. For a week, the children recorded examples of inappropriate bus behaviors.

The class then brainstormed: What can be done to make things better? They broke the responses down into lists of what children can do, what school and community adults can do, and what bus drivers can do.

Lefave and Gallagher asked the students to focus on what they themselves could do. In particular, the class would look at the issue

50

of bullying. As a way into the subject, the children discussed th___
bus worries and drew pictures and wrote stories about them.

Involving fifth graders

At this point it became apparent that older students were the ones
who were doing much of the bullying. What if, the third graders
wondered, we got some of the big children on our side? Lefave and
Gallagher identified five fifth graders who would be beneficial to the
project. The third graders invited these older students to work with
them two times a week during language arts period. Together the
third and fifth graders discussed what bullying felt like and why
some people bully other people. "The fifth graders had good insight
into why kids bully," Lefave said. Some bullies want to be cool or
want attention, and some bullies act the way they do because their
home life isn't great, the fifth graders said.

Breaking up into groups of six or seven, each group having a fifth
grader in it, children role-played bullying behavior, its outcomes,
and possible ways to prevent it. To further raise awareness of bullying behavior, the teachers had the children take a "bully test," a quiz
of yes-and-no questions from the book *Bullies Are a Pain in the Brain*
by Trevor Romain. The goal of the quiz is to get every child to
look at his or her own behavior and see how to improve it.

The children's journals, which they kept throughout the project,
showed some important learning. Some students were surprised to
learn that they had bullying tendencies. Others wrote that they hadn't
known they had the power to say "stop" to bully behavior.

To see if their work had any effect on bus behavior, the class con-
ducted a pre- and post-project survey of students, asking the same
questions each time. On most questions, students' answers showed
there was an improvement in bus climate. Most dramatically, the
percentage of third graders who said they worry on the bus dropped
from sixty-one before the project to thirty-eight after the project.

.he percentage who said that other students boss them around on the bus dropped from sixty-one to fifty.

The children also tallied up the number of incidents of behavior problems reported by bus drivers. In January and February, before the project started, the drivers reported twenty-two incidents. After the project was underway, in March and April, they reported only eleven incidents.

To mark the completion of the project, students planned a celebration called "The Bullyproofing Presentation." They wrote invitations to the mayor, the superintendent of schools, the principal, the bus drivers, and the head of the bus company; in some cases, they followed the written invitations with personal phone calls. At the celebration, which was attended by all those invited, the children greeted their guests, sang songs and read stories about school bus rides, performed their bus bully plays, and shared what they learned about preventing bus bullying.

During this first year of the bus project, the fifth graders became important and accepted members of the third graders' class community. Realizing that the third graders were watching them, the participating fifth graders acted as role models and curbed their own school bus misbehavior. In general, bullying behavior on the bus decreased and children felt safer. Students involved in the project learned to identify a problem and to think about solutions. They were energized and had many ideas for other projects.

Parents, who worried at first that the project would take away from "regular" education, became convinced that the CSL project was addressing a problem over which they felt powerless.

Bus drivers speak out

The reaction of the bus drivers, however, was another story. They were uncomfortable with the role-playing at the celebration. Feeling blamed and unsupported, they wanted their side to be heard.

Seeing the bus drivers' response, Lefave and Gallagher looked at each other and said, "We can't just leave this alone!" So Lefave signed up for an advanced CSL course, and the two colleagues started thinking about a follow-up CSL project in which bus drivers would have a role.

One thing they had learned from the first project was that the problems on the bus weren't necessarily created by the expected "troublemakers." "It was everybody," said Gallagher, describing the insight that was key to the next project.

The second year's project involved a new class of third graders and a whole class of fifth graders taught by Madeleine Carlow. The classes worked on the project twice a week during language arts. Building on the awareness that problems on the bus weren't necessarily created by the expected "troublemakers," teachers brainstormed with the children about why many children "go bananas" on the bus. Students reasoned that it had to do both with students' anonymity—they didn't have a relationship with the bus driver—and the unstructured environment of the bus. Add in morning nervousness and end-of-the-day fatigue, and the bus became the perfect place to try out rule-breaking behavior.

"Kids realized that they don't act this way in class because they know their teacher. So, what if they knew their bus driver?" said Lefave.

The children decided to interview the drivers. After brainstorming, the children came up with a list of questions. In groups of mixed fifth and third graders, divided according to which bus they took, they practiced interviewing. Then they made appointments with the eight bus drivers for interviews and picture taking. With the information from their interviews and the photos, the children made posters and hung them all over the school. "Meet the driver of the Flower Bus," said a typical poster. "His name is _____. He has a dog. He likes to travel."

The students kept journals, which they shared during "sharing time" each week. And, through role-playing, they discovered that bus driving was a hard job. They realized how distracting—and dangerous—it could be when students misbehaved on the bus.

Creating kid-friendly bus rules

Also during this second year, students focused on another important reason why children behave better in the classroom than on the bus—because the classroom has rules. Did the bus have rules?

Yes. The teachers brought in the existing bus rules to show the students, but "the kids didn't understand a word," says Gallagher. Sentences such as "Do not behave in a boisterous manner" and "If seats are not available, proceed toward the rear of the bus, remain standing in the middle aisle, and grasp a seat bar firmly," while crucial, didn't mean much to the children. So the students took on the project of rewriting the bus rules in kid-friendly language. Each mixed third-fifth grade group worked on a few of the rules, and after each group presented its work, the class came up with a final set of easy-to-understand and specific rules. About fighting, teasing, and yelling, for example, the children wrote, "Don't join in," "Ignore them," "Tell the bus driver," "Remind them of the bus rules," and "Tell them to stop."

With some funding from a $300 mini-grant from the school district, and with the help of a parent who did the graphics, the class made copies of the kid-friendly rules and distributed them to all the students in the school.

The culmination of this second year's project was "Bus Driver Appreciation Day," to which the children invited the drivers, the whole school, and the press. The children also asked the rest of the school to make appreciation posters.

The day started in the cafeteria with a breakfast of bagels, donuts, coffee, and juice (also funded by the mini-grant) for drivers and the third and fifth graders. They played getting-to-know-you games and shared the posters. "We were teaching kids the art of conversation and social interaction," said Gallagher, who was pleased to note that students gravitated toward their own bus driver.

At the end of the day, the whole school met outside on the grass. The children who had interviewed the drivers greeted them, introduced them to the school, said one thing they had learned about them, and presented them with a flower. Then the whole school gave them three cheers of "Hip, hip, hooray." "The bus drivers were beaming," said Lefave.

In assessing this second year of the bus bully project, Lefave says, "The children bought into it more than I ever imagined. They wanted to take on the world after this."

Looking back at the two years

Although this project would be suitable for any grade, Gallagher notes that it was especially appropriate for the third and fifth graders. In third grade, children are taking steps toward independence. They want the security of having adults around them, but they need to feel they have the power to make things happen. They can talk about what's bothering them; they also want to fix it. Working with fifth graders gave them something to aspire to. Conversely, the pairing allowed the fifth graders to take care of the third graders by being role models. As one fifth grader wrote: "I am learning that I should act better on the bus...since I am a fifth grader and students look up to me."

Both Lefave and Gallagher recognize positive results for themselves as well. Gallagher had a way to address the students' sometimes tearful frustration with their morning bus ride. Lefave says that because her job was to facilitate the students' process, "I didn't have to be up there lecturing all the time." Working with Gallagher also helped break the isolation of teaching.

If they were to do the project again, say Lefave and Gallagher, they'd scale back the number of activities. They feel they were overly ambitious and that the project would have been just as worthy if they had done less each year.

Finally, the North Adams team advises maintaining clear communication with school administrators about any bus behavior that requires immediate discipline. The teachers at Brayton Elementary kept careful records when children reported misbehavior on the bus and promptly relayed the information to school administrators. Not only does this ensure children's emotional and physical safety, it also addresses the school's legal obligation to act on reported incidents of harassing behavior.

Beyond its local and immediate impact of reducing incidences of bullying on the school bus, Gallagher says that the bus bully project was a small step in addressing student violence, which is so prevalent these days. "A lot of the kids doing violence have been bullied," she says. "So if we don't start here, with the little ones, look at what it can lead to."

Resources used by
Karen Lefave and Nancy Gallagher:

Froschl, Merle, Barbara Sprung, and Nancy Mullin-Rindler, with Nan Stein and Nancy Gropper. 1998. *Quit It!: A Teacher's Guide on Teasing and Bullying for Use with Students in Grades K–3.* Jointly published by Wellesley College Center for Research on Women, Educational Equity Concepts, and the NEA Professional Library.

Mullin-Rindler, Nancy, researcher and compiler. 1998. *Selected Bibliography of Children's Books About Teasing and Bullying for Grades K–5.* Wellesley, Massachusetts: Wellesley College Center for Research on Women.

Stein, Nan and Lisa Sjostrom. 1996. *Bullyproof: A Teacher's Guide on Teasing and Bullying for Use with Fourth and Fifth Grade Students.* Jointly published by the Wellesley College Center for Research on Women and the NEA Professional Library.

All of the above may be ordered from: Center for Research on Women, Publications Department, Wellesley College, 106 Central Street, Wellesley, MA 02481, (781) 283-2510, www.wcwonline.org

Romain, Trevor. 1997. *Bullies Are a Pain in the Brain.* Illustrated by the author. Edited by Elizabeth Verdick. Minneapolis, Minnesota: Free Spirit Publishing.

Wetlands as Classroom and Service Opportunity

School: Forest Avenue Elementary School, Hudson, Massachusetts

Grade level: fourth

Demographics: grades K–5, 500-plus students, suburb of Boston

Academic areas emphasized: language arts, math, science, social studies

Service theme: environmental

Project Summary

Behind the playground at Forest Avenue Elementary School in Hudson, Massachusetts, a small wetlands area serves as both classroom and service opportunity for children in Dawn Sather's fourth grade class.

Students go into the wetlands for an hour a month during the school year to monitor temperatures, identify species, track animals in the winter, and tap maple trees to make syrup in the spring.

Over the years, their explorations have spawned numerous community service learning projects. The children have organized litter cleanup days, brought second graders to the wetlands, raised money for environmental organizations at an annual school-wide Hat Day, participated in letter writing campaigns on behalf of environmental protection causes, and certified a vernal pool. Besides providing the obvious science lessons, the wetlands projects allow students to learn or practice math skills, such as measurement, arithmetic calculations, graphing, and mapping. Students keep journals, have class discussions throughout the year, and read and discuss the newsletter from a local river protection organization—all of which reinforce reading, writing, speaking, and listening skills. For specific events, children make posters or write letters to officials, getting more language arts practice.

In addition, since many of the projects involve people and organizations outside of the school, students gain experience interacting with various layers of the community, from the superintendent of schools, to local corporations, to state officials.

Working in the wetlands is a particularly suitable activity for fourth graders, says Sather, because the social studies curriculum includes study of Native Americans. By studying the wetlands, students gain personal experience with Native Americans' respect for nature. And the activities satisfy two of the goals of the Hudson school district—to use the environment in environmental education and to involve children in community service learning projects every year.

Our hands-on studying of the wetlands connects to so many areas of the curriculum. It's a service to the community and to the children, teaching them awareness of the need to protect the environment. And the children, as well as the teacher, have fun doing [the projects].

Dawn Sather, fourth grade teacher
Forest Avenue Elementary School
Hudson, Massachusetts

Project Description

It all started seven years ago when fourth grade teacher Dawn Sather jumped the fence behind Forest Avenue Elementary School in Hudson, Massachusetts. She had just returned from a course on watershed education where a trainer had asked, "Do you have wetlands behind your school?" Sather decided to find out.

When she discovered that a vibrant wetlands area did in fact exist, it was like hitting the jackpot. Here, on town-owned land, was a living, ever-changing outdoor classroom that would provide endless opportunities for learning about the environment. Sather knew that the first step was to create an easy way for students to get to the wetlands. So she went to the superintendent of schools, Sheldon Berman, a longtime proponent of socially responsible education, and asked for—and got—a gate.

Sather and her students started to explore the wetlands, using intuitive thinking to hypothesize about the things they found, such as barbed wire going through trees. "Was this formerly farmland?" they wondered. They talked about the purposes of the wetlands and identified species. By the end of the year, all of the fourth grade classes in the school were coming to the wetlands.

These days Sather, now in her thirty-fourth year of teaching, takes her class out to the wetlands for an hour on the first Tuesday of every month. Students wear long-sleeved clothes and appropriate shoes for protection from insects, scratches, and poison ivy and sumac. Working in groups of four or five, each accompanied by a parent volunteer, the children monitor plots that they adopt for the school year, measuring the depth of the water and the temperature of both the water and air. Other activities change according to the seasons. When snow is on the ground, the fourth graders take second grade buddies with them to do animal tracking. In March they tap maple trees to make syrup. In May they go "ponding," investigating water from the wetlands to find evidence of species.

And over the years, as students worked in the wetlands, environmental service projects began to present themselves.

Certifying a vernal pool

Sather likes to enlist experts from the larger community to come and talk to her class. Often an environmental CSL project grows serendipitously from that interaction. One of the first projects the fourth graders participated in emerged from a visit by Bonnie Potter, president of the Environmental Trust in nearby Bolton. Sather had invited this local environmental educator to help students discover just what they had back there behind the school. When Potter found salamander egg masses, she informed the class that their wetlands included several vernal pools, which are defined as contained basin depressions that fill with water each spring and support the activities of certain amphibian and invertebrate species.

Potter told the class that they could try to get a vernal pool certified by the Natural Heritage Program of the Massachusetts Division of Fisheries and Wildlife. Certification protects a vernal pool from real estate development. "We thought certification would be exciting," says Sather. "It had the reward of helping out Hudson, and the vernal pool would be protected."

Sather's classes began gathering the information needed to certify the vernal pool. Though the task isn't very complicated, it took the students three years because they had so many other projects going on. To get the certification, students measured the pool using balls of string, then made graphs and drawings of the outline. They took photos of salamander larva and egg masses, since one way to verify that a body of water is a vernal pool is to show that salamanders breed there. Using observation sheets and consulting their field guides, students identified salamanders and other species that may also be present in a vernal pool, such as wood frogs, fairy shrimp, leeches, dragonflies, and spring peepers. They kept records of their findings and wrote in their journals.

One of the most exciting aspects of studying a vernal pool is the annual "Big Night," the first rainy spring night when temperatures are above forty degrees. These are the conditions salamanders need for their migration to the pool, where they mate. The fourth graders and parent volunteers, equipped with cameras and cellophane covered flashlights that wouldn't disturb the salamanders, observed the migration and mating dance on the pool bottom.

"My child will always remember fourth grade because of the salamander migration," one parent said about this extraordinary event.

Students in the third year of this project assembled all the evidence into a notebook that they submitted to the Natural Heritage Program, which approved the application for certification.

"One thing just mushrooms into another"

That wasn't the end of the service learning. "One thing just mushrooms into another," says Sather about the many other projects her students have been involved in over the years.

Early on, one class discovered a local group that was working to protect the Assabet River, which is fed by the wetlands. Looking for a way to get involved with the Organization for the Assabet River

(OAR), the class made posters promoting the group's river cleanup day. This effort led to students' annual involvement with OAR through membership and fund-raising efforts, including the yearly school-wide Hat Day, when students pay twenty-five cents to wear a hat to school. The event is now organized and promoted by all the fourth grade classes in the school.

In Sather's class, the children prepare for the event by reading the book *She's Wearing a Dead Bird on Her Head!*, the story of the founding of the Audubon Society. Students then make posters and promote Hat Day to their schoolmates. After the fourth graders collect the money, the project becomes a math assignment as they tally up the money and donate half to OAR and half to the Audubon Society.

Sather's students discovered another cleanup opportunity when they noticed that litter from the playground ended up in the wetlands. The class decided a school-wide cleanup day was in order. The principal was reluctant at first, but when one of the fourth graders wrote him a letter, he changed his mind and the cleanup day took place.

Yet another project came from a classroom visit by then State Senator Robert Durand. Although the purpose of Durand's talk was to explain the difference between federal and state government, he also spoke about his interest in passing a River Protection Act. "We thought, 'This is awesome,'" remembers Sather. The children wrote letters in support of the Act, which later passed. "We feel we helped pass the River Protection Act with our letters," Sather says. Their action was the beginning of a relationship between the school's fourth graders and Durand, who now, as state secretary of environmental affairs, returns regularly to the school for environmentally related activities.

In another example of how one worthy effort leads to another, Sather applied for and won a President's Award for Elementary Science based on her work with water and wetlands. She decided to put $3,000 of her $7,500 grant toward building a wheelchair accessible boardwalk in the wetlands to give everyone in the community the opportunity to enjoy and learn from the area.

"It was a dream come true to put a boardwalk in there," says Sather. Volunteers from nearby Intel Corporation designed and built the walkway, which the town named in Sather's honor. To celebrate the boardwalk's completion, the fourth graders hosted a ribbon-cutting ceremony, inviting Intel employees, Durand, school superintendent Berman, and other representatives from the school, neighborhood, and town.

Does all this wetland activity take time away from teaching the required curriculum? Not at all, Sather has found. In fact, she realized early on that it would help her satisfy some of her state and local teaching requirements. In social studies, exploring the wetlands fosters a respect for nature that ties in nicely with the fourth grade Native American curriculum. Since the study of water is one of the mandated science curriculum areas in Massachusetts, the wetlands is a natural classroom. And studying the wetlands aligns with Hudson School District's emphasis on hands-on environmental learning and community service learning.

An ongoing exploration

On a recent sunny day in May, Sather prepares the class to go ponding. The day's effort is in preparation for Biodiversity Days in early June, a statewide attempt at species inventory. For three days in June, people young and old are invited to identify as many species as possible in their community, then forward the information to the state. The resulting catalog of species is used in efforts to prevent further losses of biodiversity in the state. Organizing Biodiversity Days in their school is the latest in the fourth graders' list of CSL activities.

The students gather their ponding supplies. Every group has a bucket, a small plastic container, plastic spoons for scooping things out, a thermometer, and a magnifying glass. Each child carries a checklist, on which he or she will be graded. The children gather at the end of the boardwalk as Sather, dressed in waders, walks out into the knee-high water. She scoops up some water in a bucket and brings it back, where it is divided among the student groups for investigation.

On her next foray into the water, Sather finds a yellow-spotted salamander egg mass and carefully shows it to the children. A few interested students hold it, crying, "It feels like slime!" When they're done investigating, students kneel close to the water and carefully return their specimen "ambassadors" to the pool.

Back in the classroom, the students write reflections in their journals and discuss their findings. Students are clearly absorbed and invested in their wetlands activity. "We're helping the community by keeping the wetlands clean and trying to stop pollution," says one student.

"We're going to be caretakers of the world soon," adds another.

Reflecting on the children's work in the wetlands, one of the parent volunteers says, "There's no classroom, no book, no slide show, no video that can teach like coming out here."

But what about schools that have no wetlands area available, no vernal pool, no woods or stream? Is this kind of outdoor hands-on learning possible? Absolutely, says Sather. "Go outside and see what's out there," she continues. "Even in city schools there's something growing in the cracks of the pavement."

Resources used by Dawn Sather:

Edelstein, Karen. 1999. *Pond and Stream Safari: A Guide to the Ecology of Aquatic Invertebrates.* Revised Edition. Ithaca, New York: Cornell Cooperative Extension.

Available through: Cornell University Resource Center, 7 Business & Technology Park, Ithaca, NY 14850, (607) 255-2080, Fax: (607) 255-9946, www.cce.cornell.edu/publications/naturalresources.cfm, E-mail: resctr@cornell.edu

Kenney, Leo P. and Matthew R. Burne. *A Field Guide to the Animals of Vernal Pools.* Westborough, Massachusetts: Massachusetts Division of Fisheries and Wildlife; Reading, Massachusetts: Reading Memorial High School Vernal Pool Association.

Available through: Vernal Pool Guide, MassWildlife, Field HQ, 1 Rabbit Hill Road, Westborough, MA 01581, www.state.ma.us/dfwele/dfw/dfwnhes.htm or

RMHS-VPA, 62 Oakland Road, Reading, MA 01867, (781) 944-8200, www.vernalpool.org/fldgide.htm

Kenney, Leo P. *Wicked Big Puddles: A Guide to the Study and Certification of Vernal Pools.* Reading, Massachusetts: Reading Memorial High School Vernal Pool Association.

Available through: RMHS-VPA, 62 Oakland Road, Reading, MA 01867, (781) 944-8200, www.vernalpool.org

Laskey, Kathryn. 1995. *She's Wearing A Dead Bird on Her Head!* Illustrated by David Catrow. New York: Hyperion Books for Children.

My biography is about the life of Mrs. E. She was born in 1917, in Fall River, Ma. Mrs. E. had six sisters and three brothers. She considered it to be a large family. She moved to Bermuda and was schooled there. Mrs. E. enjoyed math and reading. She also went to college in Bermuda.

Mrs. E. was married, but her husband passed away. Together, they had three children. She worked in the house and not outside. Her job was taking care of housework and her children.

Mrs. E. enjoys reading novels and other types of books. She is not very fond of television. But when she does watch, she likes to watch tennis. She doesn't have any friends outside the nursing home. Mrs. E. is friendly with her roommate.

I enjoyed my visit with Mrs. E. She was very friendly and outgoing. I have a better understanding of her life.

Biographies of Nursing Home Residents

School: Kiley Middle School, Springfield, Massachusetts

Grade level: seventh

Demographics: middle school, 1,100 students, urban center

Academic area emphasized: language arts

Service theme: intergenerational

Project Summary

Students from two self-contained classrooms at Kiley Middle School in Springfield, Massachusetts, wrote biographies of nursing home residents as part of an intergenerational community service learning project.

This six-week project began with the students reading *Walk Two Moons* by Sharon Creech, a story about a girl and her grandparents. The ensuing discussions about students' feelings toward their own grandparents introduced the subject of the elderly in a way that was grounded in the students' own lives. Teachers Sheryl Stanton and Lisa Dakin and support teacher Bill Limero also talked with the students about their fears and perceptions of the nursing home and its residents.

After developing and practicing interview questions, the nineteen students paired up with residents of the nursing home for the interviews. During language arts periods, they wrote the biographies by hand, then transferred them to computers for final editing. Students returned to the nursing home one more time for a celebration where they read their biographies to the assembled residents. As a result of this experience, students' perceptions of the elderly changed. Many of them said that they realized the elderly were people much like themselves, only older. For the residents, especially those without family, relating to the children was "wonderful," as one man remarked.

The main academic area addressed in this project was language arts. Students learned how to interview and how to write a biography. They learned public speaking skills and the social skills of interacting with the elderly residents. Such a project can have many natural tie-ins to history, too, since students can hear about and further explore the events or time periods that the residents lived through.

*A project like this changes students' perceptions of the eld-
erly, and it gives the elderly an opportunity to see what kids
are really like. It's an eye-opening experience for both sides.*

**Bill Limero, special education
behavior/academic support teacher**
*Kiley Middle School
Springfield, Massachusetts*

Project Description

"Don't be afraid, it's just another human being," says a Kiley Middle
School seventh grader. He's talking about what he learned from his
interviews with an elderly nursing home resident. "They're a person just like me, only older."

The student is standing with eighteen other middle schoolers in
front of Ring Nursing Home on a sunny spring day. The students
are from two student learning support rooms at Kiley Middle
School in Springfield, Massachusetts. In recent weeks, the students
have been writing interview-based biographies of the nursing home
residents. Now they've returned to the nursing home to present the
biographies. Alone or in clusters, they do last minute run-throughs
of what they've written. The students are looking forward to seeing
their biography partners again, but they're nervous about having to
read their work aloud in front of the assembled residents and staff.

When Bill Limero reports that the residents are ready for them, the
students file inside for their presentation and celebration, the culmination of their six-week long community service learning project.

The project is based on *Let Their Voices Be Heard*, a program that
Limero heard about three years ago. Developed by seventh grade
English teacher Patricia Haggerty with the support of a McAuliffe
Fellowship from the Massachusetts Department of Education, *Voices*
focuses on collecting the stories of senior citizens and veterans

and publishing them as biographies. Haggerty helped Limero bring the program to Kiley, where teacher Sheryl Stanton, who taught seventh grade English at the time, used the program with her students.

This year for the first time Limero and Stanton—who currently team teaches with Lisa Dakin—are using the project with their students, some of whom have difficulties with academics.

Preparing carefully for the visit

The teachers began the project by asking the students to read the book *Walk Two Moons* by Sharon Creech. *Walk Two Moons* tells the story of a girl who travels across the country with her grandparents. The book prompted discussions about the students' relationships with their own grandparents, their feelings, and their memories of them. Tying the discussions to the children's own lives established a basis for later discussions about what to expect in the nursing home and how to behave there. The teachers asked, "How would you want a middle school student to treat your grandparent?" Students answered, "with respect," and realized that was how they needed to treat their biography partners.

These initial weeks of discussion also helped students think about how to devise appropriate interview questions for a biography of a senior citizen, how to ask the questions, and how to write the answers with sensitivity. "What are some questions you might ask your grandparents about their past? What would you write about if you were writing about someone's life?" teachers asked the students. Students came up with four categories of questions to ask the senior citizens: family, memories of their youth, historical events in their lives, and things they would change.

After the students brainstormed questions for each category, their teachers helped them refine the questions. For example, instead of asking questions such as "What memories do you have from when you were young?" teachers encouraged students to ask more specific questions like "Who was your favorite teacher?"

Students then drew up a final list of questions and wrote one question on each page of a flip-top notebook. Students could ask any of the questions they prepared, as they judged appropriate, and were encouraged to add questions about photos or other things they noticed in the resident's room. They practiced interviewing with each other in class and at home with their families.

Sharon Waldron, the activities director of Ring Nursing Home, had come up with a list of residents who volunteered to be interviewed. Teachers matched up the students randomly, one student per resident. As they prepared to go to the nursing home for the first time to meet their biography partners, the class talked about their fears and expectations. Teachers advised that there might be some unpleasant smells, that some elderly would be in wheelchairs, and that some might be drowsy from medications. "We told the students, 'If they fall asleep, don't take it personally,'" Limero says. The teachers noted that some questions might evoke emotional reactions from the residents and that it is often good for them to express how they feel. Students could try to capture that emotion in their writing.

The class also talked about how to behave in the nursing home. Teachers asked, "What is the image we're projecting of our school when we're in the community?" They discussed what kind of language and clothes would be appropriate for the visit.

"They were so scared," Stanton recalls about her students. They worried that a resident might not like them or might yell at them. In fact, in a previous year, there was a racial comment from a resident that had to be addressed. But things went so smoothly this year that students' feelings changed dramatically after the initial visit. "Once at the nursing home, hugs and handshakes with the residents relieved the students' nervousness," says Stanton. The students quickly became comfortable, and on the way back to school, all remarked about what a great time they had.

During a reflection period back in class, students expressed concern that some residents might be lonely. Others noticed that some of the elderly were like babies in the kind of care they needed. The beginning and the end of the life cycle have similarities, they realized.

Writing, rewriting, polishing

Because many of the students had difficulty writing quickly, they had not taken notes during the interviews. So, the first step was to get the information down on paper. Many students started working right away, and then continued using their free time in the mornings to write.

"It was amazing to see them work independently and to ask for time to write," Stanton says about her students. "I didn't have to encourage them to get their work done. For an English teacher, this project is fantastic."

The following week, the class returned to the nursing home to complete their interviews. Before the visit, students talked about the fact that some of the residents might not remember their previous visit.

Then it was back to the classroom, where students completed a handwritten rough draft of their biography, which they reviewed with their teachers. They checked for holes in the information, considered whether the language was appropriate for a biography, and looked for sympathetic ways to convey painful situations in their partner's life. The students worked hard on getting it right, according to Stanton, because they wanted to make the elderly proud.

The rough drafts were entered into the computer for finer editing. Digital photos of the students with their elderly partners were also imported into the computer. Finally, each biography was printed with a photo at the top, ready to be given to the resident. In addition, all of the biographies were assembled in three notebooks—one for the school library, one for the school office, and one for Ring Nursing Home.

The presentation ceremony

On the day of the celebration at Ring, the residents gather in the activities room. The school principal is there, as well as staff from the nursing home. The students stand by their partners, then one by one they go to the podium, read their pieces, and present them to the residents. One girl also reads a poem she has written. The residents are clearly moved, more so than any of the teachers or students expected. Some residents shake their heads with emotion and approval as their biography is read. One man is disruptive, and his middle school partner tries to calm him. But most residents are quiet. Some smile broadly, others merely listen.

Many of the biographies describe the elderly as "nice" and remark about their beauty. One piece tells of a woman who had to quit work when she got married, because "that's what they did in those days." Another woman, according to her biography, "regrets getting married so young." One biography describes how "back then teachers were allowed to hit students with a ruler." The biography of one man who needs supplementary oxygen includes the cautionary plea: "Don't smoke."

Activities director Waldron says the residents enjoy their young visitors and that the project is especially good for residents who don't have many visits from family. A typical reaction is expressed by a woman who says she enjoyed doing the biographies because "I like being with kids."

Unlike some class projects, which engage some children and not others, the biography project has been a hit with all the students, according to the teachers. All the children in this year's class want to go back to the nursing home. "We had an opportunity to meet new people and learn about their life. We really enjoyed that," says one student.

A learning experience for both young and old

The teachers feel that there are many opportunities for learning in this project. The children learn how to write for an audience and then present it to them—risky endeavors for students who often struggle in school. The project lets them experience the joy and pride in doing quality work.

The elderly residents are affected, too. A relative of one resident told Stanton the next day that all the residents were talking about the project, commenting on how well prepared and well behaved the students were, how thrilling it was to see the kids.

"This project is all about perception," says Limero, explaining how both young and old often have stereotypical views of each other that change as the biography partners become acquainted. He feels that middle schoolers are especially suited for a project like this because they are willing to try things and are able to change their perceptions easily. By the end of the project, appreciation and understanding replaced the fear that many of the students once felt about the elderly. Some students even said they would help out at a nursing home.

Next year, teachers hope to start the project at the beginning of the year. They plan to add letter writing and have the children visit the nursing home repeatedly throughout the year, so that the children and elderly will be able to develop a longer-term relationship. "This project teaches kids how to be empathetic," says Dakin. "We need to give kids more opportunities like this."

Resources used by Bill Limero, Sheryl Stanton, and Lisa Dakin:

Creech, Sharon. 1994. *Walk Two Moons.* New York: HarperTrophy.

Haggerty, Patricia M. *Let Their Voices Be Heard: A Teacher's Guide.* Self-published with funding from the Massachusetts Department of Education.

Available from: Patricia Haggerty, Curriculum Coordinator, Millbury Public Schools, 12 Martin Street, Millbury, MA 01527

There is a nominal fee for printing and mailing.

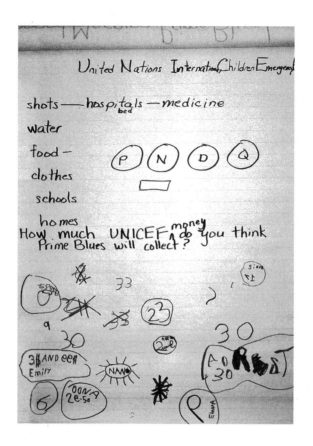

Trick-or-Treating for UNICEF

School: Greenfield Center School, Greenfield, Massachusetts

Grade level: whole school

Demographics: grades K–8, 150 students, medium-sized town in rural area

Academic areas emphasized: language arts, math, social studies

Service theme: humanitarian

75

Project Summary

Trick-or-treating for UNICEF (United Nations International Children's Emergency Fund) is a long-time Halloween tradition for youngsters at many schools nationwide. An estimated 2.5 million children in 5,000 schools carry UNICEF's orange boxes with them, collecting coins to support the international organization's work while they fill their own bags with candy. At Greenfield Center School, the independent K–8 school founded by Northeast Foundation for Children, teachers structure several academic lessons around the UNICEF project.

Beyond involving children in raising money for a worthy cause, the UNICEF project offers children a rich array of learning opportunities when done as a CSL project. Through the project, all students gain at least a rudimentary awareness of the needs of children in other parts of the world. Students also learn the basics of how UNICEF uses the money to help others. Many children, depending on their age, their interests, and the class's or school's level of involvement in the project, will develop a much deeper understanding of children's needs and UNICEF's aid.

The experience of collecting money, counting it, hearing about other classes doing the same, and learning about the purpose of this fund-raising creates a unique opportunity for children to discuss important issues. Kindergartners and first graders may reflect on basic questions such as *If someone is hungry or cold, how could we help?* and *How can I participate if my family doesn't want me to go trick-or-treating?* or *What if I forgot to ask for money for UNICEF when I went trick-or-treating?* Slightly older children might wonder *Why should we help people we don't know?* and *Why might someone not want to give money to UNICEF?* Children in the upper elementary and middle grades may have discussions around questions such as *What kind of help is most useful?* and *What responsibilities does a relatively rich country like the United States have toward poorer countries?*

The possibilities for building academic lessons from the UNICEF project are limitless as well. Math activities involve sorting and counting the money and then calculating the amount of goods and services the money will buy for children through UNICEF's programs. Social studies lessons emerge as students explore the concept of community and discuss issues of poverty. Language arts skills come into play when students write letters to UNICEF reporting how much money they raised, submit articles about their project to the local newspaper, or stand up in front of the school to describe how they sorted and counted the money. Other possible academic tie-ins range from researching geography facts about countries where UNICEF is doing emergency work to learning about the importance of vaccines, which UNICEF supplies to children in many countries.

For schools looking for a whole-school community service learning project, UNICEF offers the practical advantage of being centered on an activity—trick-or-treating—that early elementary through middle school students all can take part in. Moreover, the project is relatively simple to organize, and UNICEF provides support materials for teachers upon request.

> *There's great value in something like UNICEF being a yearly tradition, because students understand it every year at a deeper level.*
>
> **Laura Baker, principal**
> *Greenfield Center School*
> *Greenfield, Massachusetts*

Project Description

Collecting money for UNICEF is a particularly worthy CSL project because it allows children to learn about problems in the world in a concrete way and to do something about them, says Laura

Baker, principal of Greenfield Center School. "We want to build hope through ethical inquiry," Baker adds. "Trick-or-treating for UNICEF allows children to ask ethical questions. When they do projects like this, they don't feel cynical, because they see that they have the efficacy to make a difference."

Baker introduces UNICEF right before Halloween at one of Greenfield Center School's weekly all-school meetings. "What is UNICEF?" she asks. The first answer comes from a third grader, who remembers what the letters stand for. Other children share what they know. Laura talks with the children about the purpose of trick-or-treating for UNICEF and announces that the whole school will be involved in the project.

When the UNICEF boxes are handed out in individual classrooms, and when children bring them back filled with coins after they go trick-or-treating, teachers talk about UNICEF with their students again, in discussions tailored to the developmental understanding of the students. The accompanying math and social studies lessons are also geared to each class's academic skills and goals.

A kindergarten and first grade classroom

In Chris Pinney's kindergarten and first grade classroom, it's shortly after Halloween and children have done the trick-or-treating part of the project. Now they and their teacher are sitting in a circle on the meeting rug. A number of orange UNICEF boxes, filled with coins, are piled at Pinney's feet as she writes the word "community" on the meeting board. Her goal is to help the students become more aware of others and their needs.

"What is a community?" Pinney asks. Hands go up.

"A whole bunch of people," says one girl.

"A whole bunch of people doing the same thing," another child says.

"Are we a community?" asks Pinney, gesturing to show she means the class. "Is our whole school a community? How about our town? Are there communities inside of communities?"

She continues, "If our room is a community and we would like to help a bigger community, can we do it?" Heads nod in agreement.

Pinney next writes "UNICEF" on the board and leads a discussion about what the words represented by the acronym mean. The United Nations is an organization, she tells them. One boy volunteers that "international" means "countries all over the world." The children then talk about different kinds of emergencies. One kind is "if you don't have food or water," a child says. "Or if someone is badly hurt," says another. "Like when I broke my leg!" one girl chimes in, referring to an incident familiar to the whole class.

"How can this money help children all over the world?" Pinney asks, and the children brainstorm: It can pay for water, food, shots, clothes, schools, homes—all things that are important to themselves, too, Pinney points out. "You are helping kids who are a lot like yourselves," she says.

Then the children sit at several tables, and Pinney puts four paper plates and three or four UNICEF boxes on each table. The students' task is to sort the coins by denomination. Pinney's goals here are coin recognition and sorting. She says about this work, "Each year your math piece is where your kids can take it. One year I had kids who could count. That's not true yet for many students this year." After about ten minutes of sorting, the children observe which piles have the most and the least and what the different denominations are.

The class ends with a song called *What Difference Does One Little Person Make?* "What can one little person do?" they sing. "What can one little me or you do? What can one little person do to help this world?..."

A second and third grade classroom

In Terry Kayne's second and third grade classroom, both the social studies component and the math component reflect the more advanced developmental age of the students. Kayne, who has taught both kindergarten-first grade and second-third grade in her seventeen years at Greenfield Center School, notes the difference between the two age groups. "Five- and six-year-olds will do the right thing because somebody tells them to," she says. "At seven, the world is opening up." With a tradition of supporting UNICEF having been established in kindergarten and first grade, says Kayne, the second and third graders now come to it with a broader understanding that is based on a burgeoning sense of moral responsibility.

When Kayne writes the word UNICEF on the board one day just before Halloween, most of the children already know what it means. Some children can name different countries. All understand that there are children who go hungry or without clothes, medicine, or school. Their discussion of global poverty begins with what the children know best, their neighborhood. One boy mentions a homeless woman he knows of and the students talk about how sad they feel that there are people like her who are in need. They know that even within their own classroom some children have less than others. The discussion then moves on to children in other parts of the world who are living without even the most basic necessities.

After Halloween, the children bring their UNICEF boxes back to school. Some children who forgot to trick-or-treat for UNICEF raided their own piggy banks for coins to fill their boxes. Because children this age are intrigued by money, Kayne built several days' worth of activities around sorting and counting the UNICEF money.

On the first day, children empty all the boxes into a plastic bucket and weigh it, to discover they have an amazing forty-five pounds of coins. Building upon the energy and ideas of the seven- and eight-year-olds, Kayne asks the children for suggestions on how to do the task of sorting and counting. She has already designated a table for each denomination of coin. After some discussion, it's decided that each child will grab a handful of money from the bucket then go around the room depositing the pennies at the penny table, nickels at the nickel table, dimes at the dimes table, and quarters at the quarters table.

The next day, the children turn to the task of counting all the coins. With Kayne's help, they arrive at a counting procedure for each denomination—putting 100 pennies into a bowl to make one dollar, twenty nickels into a bowl to make one dollar, and so on.

As the children count, Kayne and her teaching partner, Dede Heck, go around helping the children and challenging them with math problems.

"If there are four quarters in one dollar, how many are there in ten dollars?" Kayne asks.

"I don't know."

"Well, make ten piles and we'll count them out," she says.

When all the coins have been counted, the children gather. Since they've been working for almost an hour now, Kayne helps them estimate how much money there is, putting off the job of trying to get an exact total until the next day. The class thinks they'll have about $200.

In fact, the following day, with the help of calculators, which they're just learning to use, the children arrive at their final total: $272. The children are pleased with this figure.

A fifth grade classroom

Fifth grade teacher Jane Stephenson values trick-or-treating for UNICEF because it raises awareness of the problem of poverty in the world while simultaneously offering a concrete and hopeful solution. She finds this combination especially useful for eleven-year-olds.

"Fifth graders are just starting to get a concept of personal identity," she says. And they're starting to understand issues of poverty and injustice in the world, she adds. But because it's easy for elevens to get overwhelmed and feel depressed, she doesn't emphasize the causes of injustice, stressing instead steps that can help ameliorate it.

When she distributes the UNICEF boxes before Halloween, Stephenson asks the students what they remember about UNICEF. "It's for poor kids in other countries," says one child.

"What does 'poor' mean?" Stephenson asks. You don't have money; you don't have opportunity, children answer. They discuss that poverty makes it hard for a person to be healthy and to make choices. "Why do you think we care about UNICEF?" the teacher asks, launching a discussion of everyone's responsibility, as members of a world community, to help one another. At one point, the talk turns to the students themselves and how there is a great economic range in the classroom. "My family uses food stamps," one girl says. "My mom used to be on welfare," says a boy. Stephenson then tells the students that people don't have to be rich to participate in the UNICEF project. They just have to feel a desire to help.

A few days after Halloween, the students spend a class period counting the contents of the UNICEF boxes. Using calculators, working in pairs, and checking each other's work, the children agree on $155.59 as the class total.

Meanwhile, Stephenson has written on the board some figures she found on UNICEF's website: $4.50 = one blanket; $60 = immunizations against measles for 428 kids. "If we have $155.59 and it costs $4.50 to buy a blanket so a little kid can keep warm, how many blankets do you think our class could buy?" she asks. The children turn to their calculators and someone comes up with 34.5755555.

"How would you read that number?" asks Stephenson. "What's the whole number? How many blankets is that?" Some children are lost, so Stephenson conducts a lesson on repeating numbers and how to round to the nearest whole number. Then she challenges students to use mental math for another problem using UNICEF figures: "If it costs $60 to immunize 428 kids, approximately how many kids could get immunized with the money we raised?" Children raise their hands with answers and how they got them. One child figures out a mix of blankets and immunizations. It's a concrete way for children to practice math concepts.

The next day, Stephenson talks more about what can happen with the UNICEF money. She asks the class to think big. "This is just our class," she says. "How about the money that's raised by our whole school? By our town? Just how many schools are there in our town?" she wonders. A child volunteers to look in the phone book to see how many schools are listed there.

Then Stephenson wonders what other things can be bought with UNICEF money and sends two volunteers to the computer. While the class observes, these two go to the UNICEF website and report back: "Twenty-four cents protects six kids from blindness." And so the children get a mini-lesson on how to conduct research, too.

Sharing their results

The final part of Greenfield Center School's UNICEF project involves sharing information and reflections with people outside the class. This happens on two levels: sharing with the rest of the school at an all-school meeting a few weeks after Halloween and sharing with people outside the school.

For Pinney's kindergartners and first graders, sharing with the rest of the school consists this year of three volunteers from the class describing their process of sorting the coins. They also report the total amount the class raised, an amount calculated by two third graders who were asked to do the task a few days after the younger children finished their coin sorting.

Pinney's class decides to share their work with someone outside of the school by dictating a letter to the former school secretary, Maria Lauricella, a driving force behind the school's UNICEF tradition. Pinney writes the children's words on a big sheet of easel pad paper. "We told her how much money we raised," says one girl. "And how we're helping other kids, like if they're sick." Another student reflects, "It's good to take some of your money and give it to others. You should take care of others more than yourself, like when you serve yourself last."

Meanwhile, Kayne's second and third graders decide to have one classmate stand up at the all-school meeting to describe the process they used to sort and count the coins, as well as to report their total—in weight and dollar amount. They also write about their project in the school's weekly bulletin to students' families.

Finally, Stephenson's fifth graders, besides reporting their total at the all-school meeting, choose to write a class letter to UNICEF, telling the organization how much money the class raised. They are proud of their accomplishment. "I loved counting out the money," says one student. "It's exciting how much money we collected." Another student says, reflecting on some information that UNICEF had imprinted on the orange collection boxes, "I was thinking how it says on the box that four cents buys something for children. Then if you think of the money the class and the school raised—with all that money you can do a ton."

This highlights one of the most important benefits of community service learning projects: The students learned that working as part of a community is more effective than working alone. "Adding the math component—the sorting and counting of the money, which is math made real—makes the ethical piece more concrete," principal Baker says. "If the children just pass in a box, there is no sense of how the money grew. Counting the money builds efficacy, because children see that the power of one plus one plus one is a whole lot."

Collection boxes
are available through UNICEF.

If you want to have your class trick-or-treat for UNICEF, contact the organization in September or during the summer before school starts. Call (800) 252-KIDS or visit www.unicefusa.org. UNICEF will send the collection boxes and accompanying materials to you or tell you about any distribution points for collection boxes in your local area. A video about the trick-or-treating project is available from UNICEF for a fee.

Thirteen Projects
At-a-Glance

Quilt Project

School: Hubert Kindergarten Center,
Hudson, Massachusetts

Grade level: kindergarten

Demographics: kindergarten,
200 students, suburban

Academic areas emphasized: math,
language arts, social studies, science

Service theme: humanitarian

At this twelve-class kindergarten center in a suburb of Boston, the children make baby quilts as part of a yearly community service learning project. They then present the quilts as baby shower gifts to pregnant women at a nearby homeless shelter as a way to show they care about the women and their babies.

At the beginning of the project, teachers read aloud *The Quiltmaker's Gift*, written by Jeff Brumbeau, a book that tells the story of a woman who lives on a mountain and makes quilts for the homeless people in the village. They also read *Home Is Where We Live*, by B. L. Groth, a child's account of life in a shelter.

Each child then draws on a square of fabric using fabric markers. Next, parent volunteers take the squares home to assemble them into a quilt. In recent years, some teachers have invited women from the shelter to assemble the quilts, with the school paying them a modest fee. This complements a program at the shelter that teaches the women sewing as a possible future livelihood.

Every kindergarten class also creates a book in which each child, with parental help, uses one page to introduce himself or herself to the baby who will receive the quilt. The children also write as a class to the baby, stating their hopes for the child. When all is ready, a representative from the shelter comes to the school to receive the quilts and the books, talking with each student about the quilt square and book page that the child made. Finally, the quilts and the books are presented to the women at their baby shower.

For the women at the shelter, the beautiful quilts, the homemade books, and the children's good wishes are gifts of hope. The fact that they are made by children only a few years older than the baby makes the gifts all the more precious.

For the kindergartners, the project offers a wealth of academic tie-ins. The children learn simple geometry and practice fine motor skills when they make the quilts. They practice language arts skills by reading about quilts and quilt-making and creating their own books for the newborns. Finally, learning about homelessness opens up myriad social studies questions.

Teachers add new academic or service learning components each year. "In projects like this that have longevity, you find more and more links as they go on," says Hudson CSL coordinator Mary McCarthy. The latest addition is a science unit to study the quilt fabrics—their fibers, where the fibers come from, and how the fibers get made into fabric.

And of course, the project teaches an important lesson in doing for others. As one five-year-old said, "It makes me want to do more things for other people."

Heifer Project

School: Mt. Lebanon Elementary School,
West Lebanon, New Hampshire

Grade levels: kindergarten and third

Demographics: grades pre-K–3,
300 students, small town

Academic areas emphasized:
social studies, geography, language arts

Service theme: humanitarian

In the months after Hurricane Mitch hit and nearly wiped out Honduras in October 1998, relief aid poured in from around the world. Among the aid was the livelihood-sustaining gift of a heifer, sent by a group of children at Mt. Lebanon Elementary School in New Hampshire.

Since the start of school that year, the children, a class of third graders and a class of kindergartners, had been learning about different parts of the world and what people might need when they're poor or when they've been struck by a disaster. They learned how having farm animals can help people get and stay out of poverty, and how the agency Heifer Project International provides such animals to people around the world. The two classes set a goal of raising enough money for the Heifer Project to buy one animal. But what country should get this aid?

When news hit the airwaves about the devastation in Honduras caused by Hurricane Mitch, the children had their answer. They were hearing the word "Honduras" day and night on TV, on the radio, and from their parents. Some of the older children were seeing the word in newspaper headlines. Honduras was very high in the children's awareness, even if some of the children, especially the kindergartners, had only a vague idea of where it was. The children easily decided to buy a heifer for a Honduran family who had lost their farm to the storm.

To raise the money, the children, buddying up in third grade-kindergarten pairs, made cow-shaped cookies and sold them to parents on a family night at school. When Valentine's Day came round, they made Valentine card kits—manila folders stuffed with paper hearts, packets of glitter, pieces of yarn and cloth, and other tidbits for creating original cards—and sold them to the rest of the school. Teams of third graders and kindergartners gave a presentation to every class on how a cow could help a family in Honduras and how every child could help by buying a card kit. Meanwhile, letters were sent home asking parents to support the cause by giving their child money to buy a kit. The cow cookies and card kits together netted $700, enough to buy one heifer.

Encouraged by the success of this project, the teachers, Ethel Weinberger and Pat Howe, have repeated it in subsequent years. Each year the children choose which country to buy an animal for by paying attention to media reports of poverty and other crises around the world.

Realizing that it's a stretch for kindergartners and even some third graders to understand the idea of long-term relief for countries so far away, Weinberger and Howe take every opportunity to make the abstract concepts more concrete for their students. The classes often go out to the playground where a map of the world has been painted on a hardtop area. They walk from North America to other continents to understand the idea of different places in the world. To learn about farm animals and how they can help people survive, the children take a field trip to an agricultural fair. They visit a farm where they can see milking and try their hand at it. The children read *Beatrice's Goat*, a true story of how one girl's life was changed gift of a heifer from the Heifer Project. And all year long, re ever present and often pored over in both classrooms.

result of all this learning is that the third graders develop a solid understanding of the why's and how's behind the project. Even the kindergartners, says Weinberger, come to grasp the concepts a little. As one kindergarten boy said about the Honduras effort, "A big wind came and blew their cows away. We got them another cow."

COWS

A kindergartner's drawing, done as part of the class's reflections about working on the Heifer Project.

Visits to an Alzheimer's Unit

School: Denison Elementary School,
Denison, Iowa

Grade level: first

Demographics: grades K–5,
600 students, small town

Academic area emphasized:
language arts

Service theme: intergenerational

First grade teacher Kathy Struck was on a memory walk in 1999 to honor her mother, who had recently died of Alzheimer's disease. As she walked, she got into a conversation with staff from the Alzheimer's unit of a local care center, and the idea for a service learning project was born. Why not have the first grade students visit the residents? It would do a world of good for both the older people and the children.

Every year since then, Struck and her first graders have made a monthly visit to the Eventide Care Center. Sometimes the children and the residents do art projects together. Other times they read or look at books. One time the children put on a play. One Thanksgiving everyone made paper turkeys. Sometimes the residents plan the activity, like the time they decided to play beanbag toss with the children.

For the residents, the children's visits bring comfort and joy. Though many of the residents can no longer talk, they may show that they're drawn to the children by putting out a hand or by a vocalization. The children obviously enjoy the visits, often asking afterward when they can go back.

Struck is always careful to prepare children before starting the visits each year. She explains what Alzheimer's is and reads aloud the book *The Memory Box* by Mary Bahr. This is the story of one boy's relationship with his grandfather, who has Alzheimer's disease. Sometimes the grandfather wanders off or talks to people who aren't there. Struck talks with the children about her own mother. "I tell them that there was a point when she couldn't remember me, but not because she didn't love me. It was just because of her illness." The children learn that a person can die from Alzheimer's. "At this age, you get some shocked faces when you say that. But I tell them that everyone will die sometime, and this is one way that some people die." Always, Struck makes it clear that Alzheimer's is not something the children can catch, like a cold.

The children handle the scene at the center beautifully, says Struck. They learn to ask residents their names and to talk about where they lived and what they did for a living, since people with Alzheimer's tend to remember these things when all else has faded from memory. Children also know to say their own names often because the residents might have forgotten. Lots of times the older people don't respond to what the children are saying, or they respond incoherently, but that doesn't seem to bother the children. Even during the summers, about three-fourths of the class keeps visiting the center with a family member, a sign of the bond that forms between the children and the residents, as well as a sign of parents' support for this project.

The project is a way to reinforce classroom lessons, says Struck. The artwork, the books, the projects that children bring to share with the residents are all things they've been working on in the classroom. Having to talk about them with someone outside their small circle of classmates helps the children reflect on and solidify their learning.

However, as important as academics are, says Struck, "for the children, the best part of this project is learning to accept someone different from themselves." She adds, "And then there's the sheer joy of doing something for someone else. I think they're walking away with a firm foundation for community service."

Vegetable Garden

School: St. Paul's Episcopal School,
Oakland, California

Grade level: second

Demographics: grades K–8,
270 students, urban

Academic areas emphasized: science, math,
language arts, social studies, Spanish

Service themes: intergenerational, humanitarian

For a couple of years now, second graders at this private school have been growing vegetables to sell at a weekly neighborhood food co-op. The second graders' lettuces, radishes, snap beans, and tomatoes are a small but important contribution to the co-op's offerings, and the co-op fills a real need for local senior citizens who can't easily make the trip to the nearest grocery store several blocks away.

The children grow seedlings on the sunny classroom windowsills and transplant them outside to three raised beds, which were built by parents and the school's director of service learning, Love Weinstock. Each child (or team of two to three children) cares for one plant. In groups of five, guided by a teacher, the children water the plants and record observations in their log books. The groups then take turns bringing the harvested vegetables to the food co-op to sell. The money earned ($4 to $7 each trip) is just enough to buy seeds for the next go-around.

The urban garden doesn't yield a large harvest, but it produces a variety of vegetables with staggered harvesting times. That means each student group can typically sell at the food co-op three times, gaining a fair amount of experience with the entire seed-to-market process.

Beyond teaching the obvious plant-related science lessons, teacher Kate Foley has used the project to launch a number of other academic explorations. There have been lessons on measurement, money, pricing, giving change, advertising, poster-making, healthy food choices, and Spanish vegetable names. To help children understand why the senior citizens need to buy food at the co-op, Foley has taken them for walks around the neighborhood, posing questions: Do you notice any stores? Why do you think there aren't any stores in this downtown area? Where does your family shop for food? How far away from school is that? What if you didn't have a car?

As the project comes to an end, the children celebrate their harvests and their learning. One spring they made tacos, using their own lettuce as a topping. "More children than usual chose to put some fresh lettuce on top," says Foley. "If you ask the second graders, they'll tell you that it tastes better because they grew it themselves," she adds.

Water Testing

Schools: Swift River School,
New Salem, Massachusetts, and Shutesbury
Elementary School, Shutesbury, Massachusetts

Grade levels: third–fourth, fifth–sixth

Demographics: grades pre-K–6,
200 students per school, small towns

Academic area emphasized: science

Service theme: environmental

Two teachers in the neighboring rural towns of New Salem and Shutesbury, Massachusetts, recently brought real-world significance to their students' studies of water. Why not have the children, a class of fifth and sixth graders and a class of third and fourth graders, do water quality tests for their towns' residents?

The children's service would fill a real need. Most residents in both Shutesbury and New Salem get water from their own wells. A test showing no unhealthy levels of pollutants or toxins would give a household peace of mind. Results showing questionable levels would signal a household to do further testing and take other cautionary measures—measures that could make the difference between good health and illness.

Ron Berger, the fifth and sixth grade teacher at Shutesbury Elementary, and Chris Wings, the third and fourth grade teacher at Swift River School in New Salem, got a sizeable grant from the Massachusetts Department of Education for the project. They also lined up help from a group of students at nearby Hampshire College. With these supports in place, their classes got to work.

In announcing their services to the community, the children made it clear that each household's results would be reported only to that household, since the point was to provide a service to individuals rather than to do a public exposure of residents' water quality. When the announcements went out, a total of 150 residents from the two towns responded.

The children tested two samples of water from each household: the first sample was taken when the faucet was first turned on in the morning, and the second sample was taken after the water had been running for five minutes. First, they used pH paper to test the water's acid level, then they took the samples to a lab at Hampshire College and used electronic pH meters to confirm the paper-test results.

With data in hand, the children headed back to their own class-rooms. After they graphed the results, focusing on the relationship between acid level and lead content, they prepared an individual report for each household.

"The kids really got it," says Wings. "They learned that acid in water will leach out whatever it's sitting in. They understood what contaminates water and what purifies it."

And what was the quality of the water they tested? "We basically found that we had healthy water," says Wings. A couple of households, however, did have lead on the first run, and one had lead in both the first and second runs.

Although this project was expensive and involved a partnership with a local college, teachers who are unable to secure similar funding or recruit technical help can still do a scaled-back version of the project. For example, they can have children test only for acidity, which is what Wings herself might do next time around. That information alone would be useful for households "because a high pH means you might want to test further," Wings says.

Coral Transplant Project

School: Pine Peace School,
St. John, U.S. Virgin Islands

Grade level: fifth, sixth

Demographics: pre-K–6, 100 students,
small island community

Academic area emphasized: science

Service theme: environmental

In the beautiful blue-green waters off St. John in the Caribbean, fifth and sixth graders from Pine Peace School are helping to conduct a cutting-edge experiment aimed at giving coral a fighting chance against the damages done to their habitat by human activity.

Once a month, sixteen children from this small independent school, along with their teacher Rachel Roberts and five other adults, gather on the beach with snorkels, masks, fins, and an assortment of waterproof scientific supplies. Donning the gear, the crew snorkels out to a spot in the reef where scientists have artificially attached pieces of coral to surfaces in water five to twenty-five feet deep.

This is the laboratory of the Coral Transplant Project, an investigation coordinated by Friends of the Virgin Islands National Park. The goal of the investigation is to see if transplanting coral is a feasible way to renew the organisms faster than they are destroyed. The children's job is to inspect the coral, looking for signs of growth, disease, predation, or breakage. They work in groups of four, each group monitoring half a dozen assigned colonies of coral. The children record their observations on waterproof paper and take photos of the coral with digital cameras encased in underwater housings.

Monitoring the coral is a huge thrill for the students, says Roberts. They're gaining skills and knowledge in ways that would never be possible with paper and textbook studies. Students who don't know how to swim get lessons in swimming. The entire class is instructed on proper snorkeling techniques and the use and care of snorkeling equipment. Children research and learn the ins and outs of coral— what different species look like, what preys on coral, and what new growth and diseased coral look like. They learn to tell the difference between coral broken by sea currents, by predators, and by a human hand or foot.

Roberts says the project would not be possible without parent and community support, but it's also proof of what is possible when such support is in place. The coordinator of volunteers for the Friends of the Virgin Islands National Park functions as Roberts's partner for every phase of the project. Parents and others chaperone the coral monitoring expeditions. A local scuba diver teaches the class snorkeling, and a scientist gives the students a slide show about coral. A local deli donates snacks for each snorkeling trip.

In an example of how one project often opens the door to another opportunity, Roberts's involvement in the Coral Transplant Project led to her receiving a coveted TAPESTRY science grant from the National Science Teachers Association and Toyota Motor Sales, Inc. Roberts used the grant to develop the REEF Project, an effort that supports her students' wider reef studies and activities.

To Roberts, the most heartening thing about her students' participation in the Coral Transplant Project is that they are not only helping with a study, but gaining respect for the environment and their relationship to it. "They consider themselves scientists and protectors," she says. "They can speak about why coral needs to be protected. They're making connections about how they can help the world and the future."

Books on Tape

ool: Whittier Community School for the Arts, Minneapolis, Minnesota

Grade level: fifth

Demographics: grades K–5, 500 students, urban

Academic area emphasized: language arts

Service theme: helping younger children

First graders at this K–5 school got an unusual boost in reading recently when a class of fifth graders decided to make books on tape for the younger children.

Over a six-week period in April and May, the fifth graders chose sixty books written at a first grade reading level and, with help from their teacher, parents, and community volunteers, recorded themselves reading the books. Twice a week for the rest of the school year, the two classes got together. Each fifth grader buddied up with a first grader, and the pair chose one book from the library of recorded books to read together, with the older child acting as reading tutor for the younger one. The younger child then took the book and cassette home to listen to the tape some more while following along in the book. At the next get-together, the child returned the book and tape, and the process started over again with a new reading buddy and a new book.

Although a project like this would benefit students anywhere, it filled a particular need at Whittier, where students predominantly come from low-income families. Many of the parents, struggling with long work hours and low pay, don't have enough time to read to their children, explained the fifth grade teacher, Gretchen

Stewart. She saw the project as a way for the children to be read to at home without extra time demands on their parents.

Books on Tape was a success. Not only did the first graders love being read to, but as the project went on and they gained confidence in reading, they became eager to read to their fifth grade buddies. One first grader said at the end of the year, "I'll feel sad if we leave this program. I learned how to read!"

And the fifth graders? "They really owned this project," said Stewart. She had chosen books from the school library and, with the help of a small grant, bought books especially for the project. But, not satisfied with only these choices, some children brought their own favorite books from home. And they weren't happy with a mediocre recording either. They practiced and practiced until they felt it was right. "I had to get firm to get them to put the books down," says Stewart. "And if I ran out of tapes, they were on me. They'd say, 'We got our books ready. What about your part? We need the tapes.'"

Books on Tape motivated the fifth graders to improve their own reading, dramatic reading, and speaking skills. And being in the role of teacher to younger children was an effective confidence booster for several students in Stewart's class who were reading at a lower than fifth grade level. Since everyone in the class was reading and recording first grade books, even students who were struggling academically were able to feel good about themselves, Stewart says.

Books on tape is fun! The
1st graders are respectful and kind.
It's fun teaching someone younger than
you how to do something.

Part of a fifth grader's writing about Books on Tape.

Bias in Literature

School: Memorial-Spaulding School,
Newton, Massachusetts

Grade level: fifth

Demographics: grades K–5, 400 students,
suburb of Boston

Academic area emphasized: language arts

Service theme: humanitarian

When a class of fifth graders in this suburb of Boston noticed that many of the books read by children their age had racial, gender, or other biases, they decided to take action. Wanting to help their peers spot stereotyped media messages and images, they created a pamphlet called *6 Quick Ways for Kids to Analyze Kids' Books for Bias*. The pamphlet offered guidelines in six broad areas: checking illustrations; looking at characters' roles and relationships and the story line; identifying the heroes and heroines; considering the background of the author and illustrator; noticing stereotypical images and words; and checking the copyright date.

The children modeled their pamphlet on a popular one for teachers and parents called *10 Quick Ways To Analyze Children's Books for Racism and Sexism*, published by the Council on Interracial Books for Children. The children read the adult pamphlet, discussed which ideas would be important to share with children, then worked in pairs to translate those ideas into kid language.

Instead of "Is a particular problem that is faced by a minority person resolved through the benevolent intervention of a white person?" the children wrote, "Are white people always helping people of color?" The sentence "Some infamous (overt) stereotypes of...women [are] the completely domesticated mother, the demure, doll-loving little girl or the wicked stepmother" became "Is the woman always cooking and the man always hunting? Is the girl always shown playing with dolls?"

When the writing was done, two students typed the text and did the layout. With a $500 grant secured by their teacher, Mike Feldstein, the children had a local printer make 2,500 copies of the finished product.

Next, Feldstein took the students, two at a time, to the approximately forty other fifth grade classrooms in the district to give short presentations about the pamphlet and to distribute copies.

Feldstein believes there's been a rise in bias awareness in some classrooms as a result of this project. One teacher began having her students make charts of the books they read, logging the main characters' race and gender, the author's race and gender, and other key aspects. Many teachers keep copies of the pamphlet in the room where students can easily use them.

The young activists' ultimate goal is for their peers to do something about the biases they spot. As they wrote, "If you see a stereotype, take an action. Be the one to speak out. Let the author know how you feel." They hope that by taking a stand themselves, they'll persuade other children to do the same.

Salmon Restoration

School: Leverett Elementary School,
Leverett, Massachusetts

Grade level: fifth

Demographics: grades pre-K–6,
170 students, small town

Academic area emphasized: science

Service theme: environmental

Each spring, from March to May, one end of Joan Godsey's fifth
grade classroom is transformed into a fish nursery and the students
become fish nannies as they raise baby salmon destined for release
into a local river. Their project is part of a regional effort involving
nineteen schools—and counting—to reintroduce Atlantic salmon
into local tributaries of the Connecticut River, from which they've
been absent for 200 years.

Hatching and raising baby salmon is a big responsibility, as Godsey's
students find out. From preparing the fifty-gallon aquarium that will
receive the salmon eggs provided by a nearby salmon station, to
releasing the young inch-long salmon into a nearby river two months
later, attention to detail is key to keeping the fragile fish alive.

Each day, one student is assigned to monitor the temperature of the
water. Another student tests the water's ammonia level. As the eggs
hatch, students constantly skim off the filmy by-product that rises to
the water's surface so the nitrate level in the water doesn't get too
high. Feeding the babies needs to begin at precisely the right time.
Feeding too soon in the life cycle can upset the chemical balance in
the water, and feeding too late can starve the babies. When it's finally
time to release the salmon into the river, the students scoop the

salmon fry, three or four at a time, into paper cups, then wade out to look for the right spot. The water should be shallow and clear and there should be a layer of gravel where the salmon fry can burrow and hide from predators. When they find a perfect spot, the children gently place the fish into their new home.

Such care gets results. One recent year, Godsey's students successfully hatched and released close to ninety-nine percent of their approximately 350 eggs. The environmental group Trout Unlimited and the U.S. Department of Fisheries and Wildlife, the organizers of the salmon project, are pleased with the results. They hope that the efforts of Godsey's students and others will help restore the salmon population to the level it was at before pollution and dam construction eliminated the species from the region.

A project like this naturally generates a wealth of learning about fish—Godsey's students can spew more facts about salmon than many adults learn in a lifetime. "We're helping this species be not extinct," says one fifth grader. "That's important because if one species disappears, the whole food chain breaks up." But students also learned larger lessons about protecting the environment. Another student talks about how the project has changed her as a

person. "When I'm an adult, if I want to pave my driveway, I would ask, 'What would I hurt?'"

"It gives us a feeling of responsibility," says another student about doing projects like this. "It feels like we're actually helping the community."

Student-Run Business

School: Rochambeau Middle School,
Southbury, Connecticut

Grade level: seventh

Demographics: middle school,
600 students, suburban

Academic area emphasized: business skills

Service theme: humanitarian

Every March and April there's a buzz of commerce in the air at this suburban school in southwestern Connecticut. That's when seventh graders in a business-focused enrichment class sell products and services to the rest of the school as a way to benefit worthy causes and learn about running a small business.

One recent year, the class created two separate businesses. In one, called "Kool Keychains," the students bought keychains shaped like everything from high-heeled shoes to footballs and resold them at a slight markup. In "Cards and Creatures," the second business, students made and sold two products—business cards for teachers and beaded ornamental creatures. The two businesses brought in $250. The class gave a portion of this to Rainbow House, a local safe house for abused children; a portion to a local dog pound; and a portion to that year's Special Olympics to be held in Tanzania.

The students are the decision-makers and do all the hands-on work, from conceiving of the enterprises in the fall to evaluating success after the March-April selling season. This intense level of engagement allows students to learn in depth about running a business and to practice a wide array of academic skills, says their teacher Monita Leavitt. Leavitt invites business owners to talk with the class, and the students study the stock market, read business magazines, and analyze successful ventures. This exposure helps the students decide what kind of business of their own to launch. The students also learn how to increase their chances of success. For example, they conduct market surveys to see what colors, styles, flavors, and music their schoolmates prefer. Advertising comes in the form of posters, intercom announcements, messages in the daily morning memo that's read to all students, and word of mouth. And as in the real world, the students often adjust prices partway through the selling season to move inventory or attract repeat customers.

When it comes time to choose the beneficiaries of their earnings, the students typically start by brainstorming a huge list. Then they do research on potential recipients and hold many discussions before finally taking a vote.

Through it all, students learn that there's a lot more to running a business than offering a product or service for sale. In reflecting on the project, one student talked about the importance of discovering customers' unique needs. Others mentioned the need to take risks and the importance of catching a fad. And amidst the hustle and bustle of money and commerce, the children always seem to keep in sight their project's goal of helping others. As one student said of Rainbow House, the shelter for abused children, "We thought the children deserved to live in a nice place. We hope to help make Rainbow House an even better place than it is."

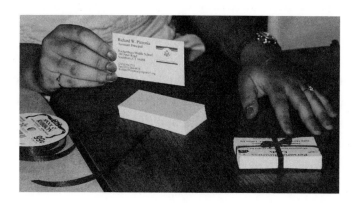

Multi-Site Community Service Learning

School: Discovery School,
Richmond, Indiana

Grade levels: sixth, seventh, eighth

Demographics: Grades 1–8,
150 students, small city

Academic areas emphasized: math,
language arts, science, social studies

Service theme: intergenerational

Tuesdays are different at Golden Rule Nursing Home. For an hour and a half in the afternoon, the place is filled with the energy of nine middle-school age students from nearby Discovery School. This week they hold a tea party. Next week they may put up decorations. Another week they may read to residents or take dictations of letters.

The residents clearly look forward to these afternoons. Even the ones who can no longer do much physical activity or carry on a conversation often come to sit with the students simply to be near them.

At the same time that these students are volunteering at the nursing home, six other groups of middle-school age students from this small public school are helping out at sites around Richmond: an arboretum, horse stables at a local college, two Head Start classrooms, an educational environmental center, an elementary school, and a second grade classroom at their own school. The students' tasks vary from site to site, ranging from mulching trails, to raking horseback riding rings, to reading with young children.

These weekly expeditions are central to the middle school curriculum at Discovery School, where students are graded as much on personal growth as on math, language arts, science, and social studies. All fifty-plus sixth through eighth graders and a few fifth graders take part in the service learning. They sign up for a site at the beginning of the year. For the rest of the year they stay at the same site, an arrangement that allows students to learn their job well and see the benefits of their efforts over time, says teacher Lisa Burkhardt, the main coordinator of the project.

Staying at the same site also allows students to form lasting relationships with the people or sites they work with. One student who worked at the nursing home arranged on her own to have her church youth group visit the residents during the winter holidays. A boy who worked at the horse stables brought his mother and sister there to volunteer.

One thing for teachers to keep in mind if they want to organize a similar effort, says Burkhardt, is finding sites with supervisors who are good with children. On site, Burkhardt and the other teachers act as aides to the site supervisors, who take on the primary leadership role. It's also important that supervisors and teachers feel comfortable communicating with each other so they can easily deal with any problems that might arise.

Burkhardt also notes the cost of a project like this. To take the children to and from the half dozen sites, the school hires a bus at a cost of seventy dollars a week. So far the school has been able to raise all the money needed in a twice-yearly appeal, with contributions coming mostly from the local VFW and a local hospital's education foundation.

The students clearly value service learning at Discovery. In an evaluation students do at the end of the school year, seventy-five percent pick service learning as one of the four most meaningful things they did, says Burkhardt.

As one eighth grader wrote, "It doesn't matter where or how you help people, as long as you do. Because if no one gives help, no one will get help."

From Student Essays about CSL at Discovery School:

"I enjoy giving to the community and I think that residents really enjoy this too...now they have a compassionate friend."

"I chose a daycare because I love working with little kids...Community service is a good idea because we get to set a good example and help teach."

"I really love to do service learning. I feel that it helps me to gain responsibility, and I especially love volunteering at Parkview Elementary because I enjoy working with children."

"The next place that I went to was a horse stables called Sunrise where we had several jobs. One was where we went looking for a reason why the electrical fence wasn't working and we found a big tree on it. It took four of us to carry it to the stable."

"I enjoy working with the children at the Head Start. They are very interesting and it brings on many challenges for me...[W]orking with the children...helps me with my attitude and the way I am with others in my community."

Voter Registration and Awareness Drive

School: Great Falls Middle School,
Montague, Massachusetts

Grade level: eighth

Demographics: middle school,
260 students, small town

Academic area emphasized:
social studies

Service theme: public policy

In the fall of 1996, as eighth graders at this school in western Massachusetts studied the presidential election, they learned that low voter turnout was a common problem in modern U.S. elections. When they realized that it was a problem in their own community, they decided to do a voter registration and awareness drive.

For two days, the eighty-seven middle school students set up booths on the village green and outside the grocery store, post office, and bookstore. They decorated the booths with signs saying things such as "Vote For Me Today; I'll Vote For You Tomorrow" to remind the public that young people counted on adults' participation in the voting process and were invested in the future. They passed out small U.S. flags that they made themselves with "Vote on November 5th" written on the back. They provided voter registration forms and instructions on where to send the forms. And they passed out a survey that they created about the candidates and key election issues. To get the word out about their booths, they advertised through flyers, the local newspaper, and the local cable channel.

"This was a meaningful project because ours was a community that wasn't very politically active," says teacher Lisa Greco, who organized the drive. The event was part of a ten-week unit on the presidential election that she taught with an interdisciplinary team of teachers. Greco feels the public survey was particularly powerful because it allowed students to see where their community stood on contemporary issues, and it allowed the community to see that its young people cared about the election. Although the survey questions, which covered topics from crime control to abortion, aroused discomfort in some passersby, the feedback was generally positive. Many who stopped at the booths said it was wonderful to see young people informed and involved in what was going on in the country.

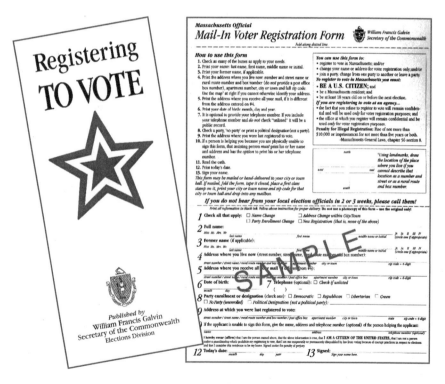

If your class would like to launch a voter registration drive, contact your county or town clerk's office to get voter registration forms and find out about rules for registering voters.

Besides the voter registration and awareness drive, the ten-week unit included a host of other studies and activities. Students read articles about the upcoming elections and wrote responses, learned about the electoral college, studied the history of elections, and held a school-wide mock election.

The learning that took place was priceless. "Students learned how you can participate in the democratic process, how you register to vote, and why it's important to vote," says Greco. "They learned what true citizenship is all about."

Hunger Awareness

School: Lincoln Magnet School of Discovery, Springfield, Massachusetts

Grade level: whole school

Demographics: grades K–5, 450 students, urban

Academic areas emphasized:
health, math, science, language arts

Service theme: humanitarian

The 450 students of this magnet school that focuses on medical science and community service learning recently joined the fight against hunger and poor nutrition by serving soup in some very special bowls.

Lincoln Magnet School's project, called *Kids Feeding Kids*, was inspired by Empty Bowls, a national anti-hunger project. At Lincoln, teachers enlisted local potters to make unglazed ceramic bowls in a variety of shapes. The students decorated and glazed the bowls and then had them fired. Finally, on a designated day, a contingent of students set up tables to sell the bowls at Baystate Medical Center, across the street from the school. For five to ten dollars, buyers not only got a beautiful, individually crafted bowl, but also got a lunch of soup from the hospital kitchen. This effort, along with similar bowl-selling events that students put on at other sites around the city, brought in about $6,000. The students used some of the money to buy household items for care packages to distribute to the city's shelters and gave the rest as a cash donation.

Kids Feeding Kids was much more than just a fund-raiser, though, says Lincoln's CSL coordinator and art resource teacher Michele Hebert. "We wanted to educate the community on how to raise healthy kids as well as heighten the level of awareness of the hunger issue." And teachers wanted to use the project to reinforce what students were learning in school about health and nutrition.

Thus blossomed a rich assortment of tie-in activities involving a variety of community partners. One fifth grade teacher used a Tufts University report about hunger in Massachusetts to teach math and reading lessons. With information from the report, her students also wrote and produced skits that were videotaped and shown to the rest of the school during morning broadcast. Students in another class, with the help of the educator who is the Christa McAuliffe Fellow of Massachusetts, wrote poems to reflect how their views of hunger and poverty changed as a result of doing the project. The physical education teacher, with support from the local electric company, organized a Walk for Hunger. Meanwhile, students from a nearby high school came to help some Lincoln students write a pamphlet on nutrition that was distributed to the community. Students from a local middle school linked up with classes at Lincoln to exchange letters about health topics and to do joint science experiments on infection control. And students in the after-school program wrote and produced plays about hunger.

"This was a truly integrated unit of study," says Hebert. In addition to helping meet a need in the community, the project gave students an exceptional opportunity to interact with one another. "The children learned that they are unique individuals who can contribute their ideas and talents to the school and community," Hebert says.

BOWLS, BOWLS, BOWLS

Conclusion
Focusing on What's Really Important

This book neared completion in the immediate aftermath of the World Trade Center and Pentagon attacks of September 11, 2001. During that time, I watched us as a nation start to re-examine priorities. Like someone who has just received a diagnosis of a life-threatening illness, we discarded the superficial trappings of life and focused on what was really important: our children, our families, and our communities. I realized that no matter what is happening in our country or world, there are certain things we still want—perhaps now more than ever—for our children. We want them to feel connected to the people around them where they study and live. And, we want them to be good people.

But most immediately, we want our children to be safe. In the wake of September 11th, we remember other tragedies such as the shootings at Columbine High School in Colorado. As a nation, we decry violence in our schools, whether it is a large-scale tragedy like at Columbine or a single student bullying another. School violence harms innocents at a time and place where they should be safe.

As the examples in this book illustrate so well, community service learning fosters caring. It helps children feel whole and connected to their schools and communities. It is a powerful antidote to isolation and alienation, and in this way it helps prevent violence. As the U.S. Department of Health and Human Services notes in its report *Youth Violence: Lessons from the Experts,* young people who feel connected to families, schools, and communities are at lower risk for violence.

CSL is a gift of hope. Yes, it is but one small part of the solution to violence. But as Marian Wright Edelman, founder and president of the Children's Defense Fund, points out, all the small actions that we take are important. "We must not," Edelman says, "in trying to think about how we can make a big difference, ignore the small daily differences we can make which, over time, add up to big differences that we often cannot foresee." As the world struggles to ensure a more peaceful future, engaging children in CSL is more relevant and worthwhile than ever.

Ideally, CSL should be a journey. On that journey, all students should have the opportunity to experience CSL every year of school. The journey begins with one step—one teacher in one school beginning one project. I hope you will feel inspired to take that step.

Community Service Learning Resources

Organizations

Corporation for National Service

Created in 1993, this federal corporation administers the Learn and Serve America program, which provides grants and other assistance for creating new CSL programs, replicating existing programs, and providing training and development to staff, faculty, and volunteers. The corporation also administers the National Service-Learning Leader Schools Program, an initiative that recognizes middle and high schools for their excellence in service learning. These schools then help other schools develop service learning opportunities for students.

1201 New York Avenue, NW, Washington, DC 20525
(202) 606-5000, www.cns.gov
E-mail: webmaster@cns.gov

National Service-Learning Clearinghouse

A project of the private, non-profit center ETR Associates, this clearinghouse collects and disseminates information and materials related to service learning for Learn and Serve America grantees and other programs involved in service learning.

ETR Associates
PO Box 1830, Santa Cruz, CA 95061
(866) 245-SERV (7378), TTY: (831) 461-0205, Fax: (831) 430-9471
www.servicelearning.org

One page of this organization's website lists funding opportunities and grant writing resources that may be helpful for educators seeking support for CSL activities.
www.servicelearning.org/res/links/funding.php

National Youth Leadership Council

This national non-profit organization is a leading advocate of service learning. It offers training, clearinghouse services, materials and curricula, technical assistance, program development, and speakers for conferences and forums.

1667 Snelling Avenue North, St. Paul, MN 55108
(651) 631-3672, Fax: (651) 631-2955, www.nylc.org
E-mail: nylcinfo@nylc.org

Learning In Deed

This W. K. Kellogg Foundation initiative works with teachers, administrators, community leaders, parents, students, policymakers, and national leaders to engage more young people in CSL. It does this by creating demonstration projects, developing policy, promoting effective leadership, and communicating the best CSL practices in grades K–12. The initiative includes the National Service Learning Partnership, a membership organization that aims to help members share knowledge and improve practices.

W. K. Kellogg Foundation
1 Michigan Avenue East, Battlecreek, MI 29017-4058
(202) 778-1040, www.learningindeed.org

Compact for Learning and Citizenship

(Housed at the Education Commission of the States)

This is an organization of chief state school officers, district superintendents, service learning professionals, and others who support service learning. Members are committed to linking school-based service and service learning to K–12 curricula and to organizing schools so that they can best use community volunteer efforts.

707 17th Street, #2700, Denver, CO 80202-3427
(303) 299-3600, Fax: (303) 296-8332, www.ecs.org/clc
E-mail: ecs@ecs.org

National Helpers Network

Established in 1982 as part of the Graduate School and University Center of the City University of New York, this organization offers service learning program models, workshops, personal assistance, and curriculum materials for teachers using CSL at the middle school level.

875 Sixth Avenue, Suite 206, New York, NY 10001
(212) 679-2482 or (800) 646-4623
Fax: (212) 679-7461, www.nationalhelpers.org
E-mail: info@nationalhelpers.org

Constitutional Rights Foundation

This non-profit, non-partisan organization is dedicated to educating America's young people about the importance of civic participation in a democratic society. It offers annual Maurice G. Robinson Mini-Grants for CSL projects. It also provides materials and training to teachers, coordinates civic participation projects in schools, and organizes student conferences and competitions on the subject of civic participation.

601 South Kingsley Drive, Los Angeles, CA 90005
(213) 487-5590, Fax: (213) 386-0459
www.crf-usa.org

Books and Other Printed Materials

Wade, Rahima C., editor. 1997. *Community Service Learning: A Guide to Including Service in the Public School Curriculum.* A volume in the SUNY series, Democracy and Education, edited by George H. Wood. Albany, New York: State University of New York Press. Paper, $23.95.

This book discusses the components of quality service learning programs and offers models of service learning programs at the elementary, middle, and high school levels. It then shares stories of service learning involvement from students, agency members, and administrators, before ending with a reflection on the future of service learning in public schools.

Kinsley, Carol W. and Kate McPherson, editors. 1995. *Enriching the Curriculum Through Service Learning.* Alexandria, Virginia: Association for Supervision and Curriculum Development. Paper, $18.95.

In this book, twenty-one K–12 teachers, administrators, students, leaders of youth-service organizations, and university faculty reflect on and share their service learning stories. The stories focus on how CSL can enliven learning.

Lewis, Barbara A. 1998. *The Kid's Guide to Social Action.* Minneapolis, Minnesota: Free Spirit Publishing. Paper, $18.95.

Most suitable for upper elementary grades and older, this book offers step-by-step guides for taking social action, covering skills such as letter-writing, faxing, e-mailing, doing Internet searches, interviewing, making speeches, taking surveys, raising money, and getting media coverage. It includes sample petitions, proclamations, letters, and news releases that can be adapted; listings of relevant social action groups and government offices; and real stories of children and teens who are taking action to improve communities at home and around the world.

Joining Hands Community Service-Learning Resource Kits. Developed by teams of public school teachers, student teachers, and community agency members and reviewed by Rahima C. Wade. Iowa City, Iowa: University of Iowa Audiovisual Center. $99 for a complete kit or $35 for an abbreviated version.

These kits are designed to help teachers and students develop CSL projects in various areas of concern, from protecting the environment to reducing poverty and hunger. A primary (grades K–3) and intermediate (grades 4–8) kit is available for each area of concern. Each kit includes project ideas, reflection questions, curriculum connections, children's literature books and resource books relevant to the kit's topic, and agencies and organizations that can facilitate research and activities.

The University of Iowa
Service-Learning Department
215 Seashore Hall Center, Iowa City, IA 52242-1402
(800) 369-IOWA (4692), Fax: (319) 335-2507
Order online: www.uiowa.edu/~avcenter/

Writer and artist Pamela Roberts lives in western
Massachusetts. She became interested in community
service learning when her two children were students at
Greenfield Center School, the independent K–8 school
founded by Northeast Foundation for Children.
Roberts has a BA in Asian studies from Cornell
University. She has written articles for the NEFC
newsletter, Responsive Classroom,
and for the NEFC website,
www.responsiveclassroom.org.